Way to Go, Coach!

A Scientifically-Proven Approach to Youth Sports Coaching Effectiveness

Second Edition

Ronald E. Smith

University of Washington

Frank L. Smoll

University of Washington

Warde Publishers, Inc.

Portola Valley, California

Warde Publishers, Inc.
3000 Alpine Rd.
Portola Valley, CA 94028
(800) 699-2733

ISBN 1–886346–07–0

Printed in the United States of America
10 9 8 7 6 5 4 3 2 1   05   04   03   02

Design: Detta Penna; Composition and paging: Penna Design and Production.

Dedicated to two former Ripon College coaches,

Kermit "Doc" Weiske

and the late

John M. Storzer

who fostered athletes' personal growth

as well as athletic excellence,

and to the countless coaches

who make it possible

for youngsters

to enjoy the benefits

of sport participation

Contents

Part 1
Developing a Coaching Philosophy 1

1 Sports and the Developing Young Athlete 3
Why Is Play So Important? 3
Why Youth Sports Continue to Grow 4
The Pros and Cons of Youth Sports 6
Sport CAN Build Character! 8

2 Youth Sport Objectives and Values 11
Kids Are Not Pros! 12
What Youth Sports SHOULD Be About 13
Is Winning Really the Only Thing? 15
The Real Meaning of Winning 16
Youth Sports and the Bigger Picture 18

Part 2
Becoming a Better Coach 21

3 Sport Science and the Youth Coach 23
Why Coaches are Important 23
The Psychology of Coaching 24
Positive Versus Negative Approaches to Coaching 25
Scientific Evidence Supports the Positive Approach 28

4 Increasing Your Coaching Effectiveness 31

Using the Power of Reinforcement 32

A Positive Approach to Mistakes 35

Maintaining Order and Discipline 38

Dealing with Team Rule Violations 40

Building Team Unity and Cohesion 41

Teaching Sport Skills Effectively 43

Communication and Self-Awareness 44

Summary of Coaching Guidelines 46

Part 3

Performance Enhancement Skills for Young Athletes 49

5 Systematic Goal Setting to Increase Motivation and Performance 51

How Goal Setting Affects Young Athletes 52

Keys to Effective Goal Setting 52

Some Pitfalls to Avoid 57

Putting Goal Setting to Work 57

6 Counteracting Stress and Teaching Mental Toughness 61

Understanding Athletic Stress 62

How Stress Affects Young Athletes 63

Mental Toughness as Teachable Skills 65

Reducing Stress and Building Mental Toughness 66

7 Mental Imagery and Performance Enhancement 81

How Imagery Improves Performance 82

Introducing the Power of Imagery to Athletes 84

Incorporating Imagery Training into Your Practices 85

Mental Preparation for Competition 87

Part 4
Health and Safety Considerations 89

8 *Physical Development* 91

Factors That Influence Body Characteristics 92

Patterns of Physical Growth 94

Changes in Physical Abilities During Childhood and Adolescence 97

Should Boys and Girls Compete Against Each Other? 99

The Growing and Maturing Skeleton 99

Sport Participation and Physical Maturity 100

The Early Maturer 101

The Late Maturer 103

The Body of Today's Young Athlete 104

9 *Training and Conditioning* 105

Shaping Up for Competition 106

Some Basics in Conditioning Programs 118

Choosing the Right Conditioning Program 120

Drugs and the Young Athlete 123

10 *Sport Injuries* 127

What Is a Sport Injury? 127

Things NOT to Do if Injured in Sport 129

Things to Do When Injured 130

Preventing Sport Injuries 131

Be Prepared for an Emergency 133

When Injury Prevents Participation 134

Can You Be Sued? 135

Part 5

Coaching Challenges and How to Deal with Them 139

11 *Approaches to Dealing with "Problem Athletes" 141*

The Uncoachable Child 142

The Spoiled Brat 144

The Low Self-Esteem Child 145

The Hyperanxious Child 146

The Withdrawn Child 147

12 *Relating Effectively to Youth Sport Parents 149*

Roles and Responsibilities of Parents 149

Fostering Open Communication with Parents 154

Dealing with "Problem Parents" 155

Avoiding Problems with a Preseason Parent Meeting 158

13 *What to Do If . . . 167*

Gaining Athletes' Respect 167

Should Kids Ever Be Cut? 168

What If a Child Wants to Quit? 169

Unusual Disciplinary Problems 170

Dealing with a Tough Loss or Losing Streak 171

Dealing with a Winning Streak 172

Trophies and Other Awards 173

Misbehavior by Other Coaches 174

Coaching Your Own Child 174

Coaching and Family Life 175

A Final Word 176

References 177
Coach's Clipboard: A Summary of Key Principles 180
Index 203

Part 1

Developing a Coaching Philosophy

Sports and the Developing Young Athlete

Millions of adults give unselfishly of their time and talents to provide organized sport experiences for children. This book has been written for you, the youth sport coach, because sport participation has great potential for improving the growth and personal development of children. There is no question that sports are important to youngsters and that coaches can have a significant long-term impact on young athletes. This book is designed to provide you with scientifically validated information that will help you make the sport experience constructive and enjoyable! Our approach is also based on the principles that are used by many outstanding coaches who have enriched the lives of athletes through their leadership skills.

All coaches do as well as they can, within the limits of their awareness. The information in these pages can increase your awareness of what you can do to improve your coaching effectiveness. This will help you deal more productively with the many opportunities and problems that can arise in youth sports.

Why Is Play So Important?

To understand the role of sports in the lives of children, we must first consider the meaning and functions of play. Animals as well as humans engage in play activities. In animals, play has long been seen as a way of learning and practicing skills and behaviors that are necessary for future survival. For example, young lions stalk and pounce on objects in their play. In children, too, play has important functions during development.

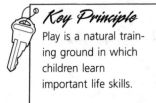

Key Principle

Play is a natural training ground in which children learn important life skills.

From its earliest beginnings in infancy, play is a way in which children learn about the world and their place in it. Children's play serves as a training ground for developing physical abilities—skills like walking, running, and jumping that are necessary for everyday living. Play also allows children to try out and learn social behaviors and personality traits that will be important in adulthood. For example, they learn how to compete and cooperate with others, how to lead and follow, how to make decisions, how to assert themselves, and so on. This occurs in free and spontaneous forms of play as well as in more structured forms, such as games and sports. Thus children's play helps them to acquire physical, social, and personal skills, serving as a kind of apprenticeship for later life.

Why Youth Sports Continue to Grow

Although children have always engaged in play, the past half century has seen the development of increasingly organized youth sport programs. How big are youth sports, and how did they get that way?

Organized youth sports in the United States actually go back to the early 1900s. The first programs were established in public schools when it was recognized that physical activity was an important part of education. Over time, sponsorship and control of some sports have shifted to a variety of local and national youth agencies. These programs have flourished, and today more children are playing than ever before.

How fast have youth sports grown? Very fast! Little League Baseball, one of the oldest programs, is a good example. It originated in 1939 in Williamsport, Pennsylvania, as a three-team league for 8- to 12-year-old boys. The program was so popular that it spread rapidly. During its 50-year anniversary season, there were some 16,000 chartered leagues in 25 countries and territorial possessions around the world, providing opportunities for more than 2.5 million boys and girls 6 to 18 years of age.

Programs in other sports have also shown rapid growth. In the United States alone about 25 million youngsters between the ages of 6 and 18 years participate in nonschool athletics. Millions more participate in interscholastic programs.

Growth of the youth sport movement has required the involvement of increasing numbers of adults. Nearly 3 million men and women volunteer their time as coaches, league administrators, and officials. As programs have become more highly organized, parental involvement has also increased. Thus, in moving from the sandlot to the more formalized programs that now exist, the youth sport explosion has touched children and adults in increasing numbers.

Several factors have contributed to the rise of organized youth sports.

- Over the years, there has been a clear recognition of the importance of wholesome leisure-time activities for children.

- The mushrooming of large cities has decreased the amount and availability of play spaces.

- Many authorities have correctly looked to sport programs as a way of reducing juvenile delinquency.

- Sport has become an increasingly central part of our culture and personal lives. We have become more fitness-minded, and the mass media have brought sporting events into the homes of virtually every family.

- Perhaps most important, sports are an enjoyable and rewarding pastime.

Growth in the popularity and scope of youth sports and in the role that they play in the lives of children is undeniable. But this expansion has generated ongoing and at times bitter debate. Serious questions have been raised about the desirability of organized sports for children. Unfortunately, answers to the questions are not simple.

Key Principle

Youth sports are deeply rooted in our social and cultural heritage. Today, nearly 25 million youngsters and 3 million adults participate.

The Pros and Cons of Youth Sports

Obviously the dramatic growth of youth sports could not have occurred if people didn't believe that participation is beneficial. Those who favor sport programs emphasize that there are many aspects of the experience that contribute to personal development. Some supporters have pointed out that sport is a miniature life situation—one in which children have to learn to cope with many of the important realities of life.

Key Principle
Supporters of organized sports point to the positive learning experiences children can have, as well as to the benefits of good adult guidance and leadership.

Within sport, children learn to cooperate with others, to compete, to deal with success and failure, to learn self-control, and to take risks. Important attitudes are formed about achievement, authority, and persistence in the face of difficulty.

Adult leadership can be one of the truly positive features of organized sport programs. Knowledgeable coaches can help children acquire physical skills and begin to master a sport. Higher levels of physical fitness can be promoted by such guidance. The coach can become a significant adult in the life of the child and can have a huge positive influence on personal and social development. Likewise, the involvement of parents can bring families closer together and heighten the value of the experience for young athletes.

On the other hand, youth sports have more than their share of critics. Coverage by the popular media is not always favorable. Because

Key Principle
Critics say that organized sports rob children of spontaneous play experiences. They focus on the excesses and abuses that sometimes occur, claiming that the programs meet adults' needs more than children's.

mistreatment of children is noteworthy, sport abuses are likely to be sensationalized and widely publicized. The media's overemphasis on the negative has understandably made some people question the value of youth sports.

Undoubtedly problems can arise in sport programs, and some of these problems have been the focus of severe criticism. *Newsweek* once published a thoughtful editorial by former major-league pitcher Robin

Roberts entitled "Strike Out Little League." This Hall of Fame baseball star pointed out that Little League Baseball can place excessive physical and psychological strains on youngsters, and that programs sometimes exist more for the self-serving needs of the adults than for the welfare of children. Experts in child development have claimed that adult-supervised and highly organized programs can rob children of the creative benefits of spontaneous play. They suggest that children would benefit far more if adults simply left them alone to their own games and activities.

Many complaints center around the role of adults in youth sport programs. Critics have charged that some coaches are absorbed in living out their own fantasies of building sport dynasties and that consequently they show little personal concern for their athletes. Opponents of youth sports maintain that parents sometimes live through their children's accomplishments and place tremendous pressure on them to succeed. When coaches and parents become more focused on themselves than on the quality of the children's experience, something is undoubtedly wrong.

The negative involvement of adults in sports has been linked to such problems as the inappropriate use of drugs for training and conditioning, physical injury due to excessive training and competition, and blatant cheating and dishonesty. The *Los Angeles Times* reported that one misguided coach injected oranges with amphetamines, then fed them to his 10- to 12-year-old football players to get them "up" for a game. The *Washington Post* carried a story about a mother who forged a phony birth certificate for her 17-year-old son so that he could star in a league for 14-year-olds.

> **Key Principle**
> A realistic appraisal of youth sports acknowledges both the benefits and the potential harm that can be done when programs are not properly structured and supervised. The key is to improve the quality of experiences for *all* youngsters.

Who's right? Are youth sports a symptom of a serious, widespread social disease? Or are they the salvation of our youth? The answer is neither. No reasonable person can deny that important problems do exist in some programs. Some of the criticisms are well founded and can be constructive. On the other hand, surveys have shown that the vast majority of adults and children involved in sports find them to be an enjoyable and valued part of their lives. The bottom line is that sport programs are what we make of them. They can become a source of joy and fulfillment in the life of a child— or a source of stress and disappointment.

We believe that sports have a strong positive *potential* for achieving important objectives. The question is not whether youth sports should continue to exist. They are here to stay as a firmly established part of our society. If anything, they will continue to grow in spite of the criticisms that are sometimes levelled at them. The real question is how adults can help ensure that participation in sports will be a positive experience for children.

What can you do to help achieve the many desirable outcomes that are possible? Perhaps the key to unlocking the potential of youth sports lies in being well informed about their psychological dimensions. We hope that the guidelines presented in this book will assist you in your role as a successful coach.

Sport CAN Build Character!

Raising our children is in large part a moral enterprise. We do our best to teach our children the difference between right and wrong. We communicate our own values to them and hope they will adopt similar values. We want them to develop positive character traits that will make them happy and contributing members of society. Our goals in this regard are shared by religious institutions, schools, youth organizations, and athletic programs. The mission of the American Youth Soccer Organization is to develop and deliver quality youth soccer programs where everyone builds positive character through participating in a fun, family environment based on the AYSO philosophies: Everyone Plays, Balanced Teams, Open Registration, Positive Coaching, and Good Sportsmanship. In the words of John Ouellette, AYSO National Director of Coaching, "Coaching youth sports should be about adults nurturing children who are playing a game, whatever that game may be, not about winning and losing."

> **Key Principle**
>
> "The greatest contribution that sports can make to young athletes is to build character. The greatest teacher of character is on the athletic field."
>
> Tom Landry,
> former Dallas Cowboys
> coach

Sport is an especially promising setting for learning the positive traits we lump under the term *character*, because it confronts children with many challenges that await them in later life. Cooperation, competition, perseverance in the face of difficulties, concern for others, self-sacrifice, and moral behavior (sportsmanship) can all be called for on any given day. Through the influence they have as important adults in children's lives, coaches can teach children to respond to these challenges in desirable ways. Important lessons of life can be learned on the athletic field and in the gymnasium.

In our attempts to teach children desirable attitudes and behaviors, it is important that we explain to children the principles or reasons behind desired actions. For example, rather than simply threatening to punish athletes for heckling opponents, coaches might help their athletes understand the Golden Rule, "Do unto others as you would have them do unto you," by asking them to consider what it would be like to be the victim of heckling—and thus encourage the youngsters to develop empathy for their opponents. This ability to place oneself in the role of another person is essential to the development of morality. Understanding and applying the Golden Rule can lead youngsters to internalize the concept of sportsmanship and consideration for others.

Youngsters learn moral behavior not only through verbal explanations, rewards, and punishments but also by observing how other people behave. They imitate their parents and peers, and they model themselves after their heroes. Because coaches are often highly admired and very important in the child's life, they are especially likely to serve as models. Without realizing it, coaches can behave in ways that teach either morality or immorality. For example, by trying to get the edge by stretching the rules, coaches can easily give children the impression that cheating is not really wrong unless it is detected, and then only to the extent that it hurts the chances of winning. When coaches bend the rules in order to obtain a victory, children may conclude that the end justifies the means. Likewise, coaches who

> *Key Principle*
>
> Sportsmanship is taught not only by teaching underlying moral principles but also by serving as a positive role model. In teaching moral values, what coaches *do* is as important as what they *say*.

display hostility toward officials and contempt for the other team communicate the notion that such behaviors are appropriate and desirable. Even when coaches preach correct values, it is essential that they themselves behave in accordance with them. Research studies with children have repeatedly shown that when adults' actions are inconsistent with their words, it is the actions, not the words, that influence children's behavior. Actions do indeed speak louder than words.

Critics of youth sports sometimes attack the competitive aspect of sports as inconsistent with the development of morality and concern for others. Some, however, dispute this position, arguing that moral development is actually furthered when moral decisions come into conflict with winning. In other words, noteworthy acts of sportsmanship often involve situations in which conduct governed by a moral principle (for example, that you should not cheat) is chosen instead of victory. When a youngster makes a decision to do the right thing rather than unfairly pursue an opportunity to succeed, we have a true demonstration of moral growth. Coaches are in a position to further such growth.

Youth Sport Objectives and Values

When children enter a sport program, they automatically assume responsibilities. But they also have rights. Adults need to respect these rights if young athletes are to have a safe and rewarding sport experience. The National Association for Sport and Physical Education's Youth Sports Task Force has developed a "Bill of Rights for Young Athletes." Here are the rights identified by these medical doctors, sport scientists, and national youth sport administrators:

Bill of Rights for Young Athletes

1. Right to participate in sports.
2. Right to participate at a level commensurate with each child's maturity and ability.
3. Right to have qualified adult leadership.
4. Right to play as a child and not as an adult.
5. Right to share in the leadership and decision making of sport participation.
6. Right to participate in safe and healthy environments.
7. Right to proper preparation for participation in sports.
8. Right to an equal opportunity to strive for success.

9. Right to be treated with dignity.

10. Right to have fun in sports.

This "bill of rights" provides a sound framework for fulfilling adult responsibilities toward young athletes. But as an important first step to guaranteeing these rights, coaches must have an understanding of the various models of sport as well as the kinds of objectives they hope to achieve. Sport models and goals are the focus of this chapter.

Kids Are Not Pros!

An important issue is the difference between youth and professional models of sport. The major goals of professional sports are directly linked to their status in the entertainment industry. The goals of *professional* sports, simply stated, are to *entertain* and ultimately to make *money*. Financial success is of primary importance and depends heavily on a product orientation, namely, *winning*. Is this wrong? Certainly not! As a part of the entertainment industry, professional sports have tremendous status in our society.

In the professional sport world, players are commodities to be bought, sold, and traded. Their value is based on how much they contribute to winning and profit-making. They are the instruments of success on the field and at the box office, and they are dealt with as property or as cogs in a machine. As a tearful Willie Mays said on being traded by the San Francisco Giants late in his career, "All they seem to care about is what you did for them yesterday and what you can do for them tomorrow."

Professional athletes are often glorified by the media to create an image intended to generate interest in the team and to draw paying customers. However many professional athletes feel that little real concern is shown for them as human beings or as contributing members of society. For example, several professional teams have reportedly turned deaf ears to reports of drug abuse by star athletes as long as the athletes continued to perform well.

The professional coach's job is to win. Those who don't, usually join the ranks of the unemployed rather quickly and unceremoniously. No gold watches for years of service, either! A win-at-all-costs philosophy is required for advancement and, indeed, survival. Professional

Key Principle

Professional sport is a commercial enterprise in which success is measured in wins and financial revenues. In a developmental model, sport is an arena for learning, where success is measured in terms of personal growth and development.

coaches do not receive bonuses for developing character. Their primary function is to help the franchise compete successfully for the entertainment dollar. As emphasized by veteran NBA coach Pat Riley, "Nobody is ever above the business of what this whole league is about, which is money."

The *developmental model* of sport has a far different focus. As its name suggests, the goal is to develop the individual. The most important product is not wins or dollars, but, rather, the quality of the experience for the child. In this sense, sport participation is an *educational process* whereby children can learn to cope with realities they will face in later life. Although winning is sought after, it is by no means the primary goal. Profit is measured, not in terms of dollars and cents, but in terms of the *skills* and *personal characteristics* that are acquired.

Sometimes these two athletic models get confused. Most of the problems in youth sports occur when uninformed adults erroneously impose a professional model on what should be a recreational and educational experience for children.

What Youth Sports SHOULD Be About

Coaches, like young athletes, involve themselves in sports for many reasons. Youth sport objectives can range from simply providing a worthwhile leisure-time activity for children to laying the foundation for becoming an Olympic champion or a professional athlete. Of course there are many other goals that may well be more appropriate. Some of them are physical, such as attaining sport skills and increasing health and fitness. Others are psychological, such as developing leadership skills, self-discipline, respect for authority, competitiveness, cooperativeness, sportsmanship, and self-confidence. These are many of the positive attributes that fall under the heading of *character*.

Youth sports are also an important social activity in which children can make new friends and acquaintances and become part of an ever-expanding social network. Furthermore, sports can serve to bring

Key Principle

Among the many benefits that children can derive from sports, perhaps the most important is simply to have fun.

families closer together. Finally, of course, youth sports are (or should be) just plain FUN!

Fun. A term we use a lot. But what is it? Certainly it's easy to tell when people are having fun. They show it in their expression of happiness, satisfaction, and enthusiasm. Being with others, meeting challenges, feeling the drama of uncertain outcomes, becoming more skilled—all of these add to the fun of sports. In the words of an 8-year old girl, "Fun is when I'm doing something that makes me happy just to be doing it, like playing tennis."

Winning also adds to the fun, but we sell sports short if we insist that winning is the most important ingredient. In fact, several studies reported that when children were asked where they would rather be—warming the bench on a winning team or playing regularly on a losing team—about 90% of the children chose the losing team. The message is clear: The enjoyment of playing is more important to children than the satisfaction of winning.

The importance of having fun is also shown in other scientific studies. A sport psychologist, Dr. Daniel Gould, summarized the results of two surveys conducted in the United States and Canada. The studies indicated that young athletes most often say they participate in organized sports for the following reasons:

• To have fun.

• To improve their skills and learn new skills.

• To be with their friends or make new friends.

• For thrills and excitement.

• To succeed or win.

• To become physically fit.

Does your popularity as a coach depend on your won-lost record? No! In one of our own studies, we found that teams' won-lost records have nothing to do with how well young athletes liked the coaches they played for or their desire to play for the same coach again. Interestingly, however, success of the team was related to how much the children thought their parents liked the coach. The children also felt that the won-lost record influenced how much their coach liked them. It appears that, even at a very young age, children begin to tune in to the adult emphasis on winning, even though they do not yet share it themselves. What children do share is a desire to have fun.

One of the quickest ways to reduce fun is for adults to begin treating kids as if they were varsity or professional athletes. We need to keep in mind that young athletes are not miniature adults. They are children, and they have the right to play as children. Youth sports are, first and foremost, a play activity; and children deserve to enjoy sports in their own way. In essence, it is important that programs remain child-centered and do *not* become adult-centered. In the words of major league baseball manager Sparky Anderson:

> It's a disgrace what we're doing in the United States and Canada. We're asking kids to compete to win. Why not ask them to compete to have fun? We're trying to build our own egos on little children.

Whatever your objectives may be, it is important that you become aware of them. And you must realize that none of these objectives can be achieved automatically as a result of mere participation in sports. Simply placing a child in a sport situation does not guarantee a positive outcome. The nature and quality of the program, which are directly dependent on your input, are prime factors in determining benefits.

Is Winning Really the Only Thing?

During his years as coach of the Green Bay Packers, Vince Lombardi created a professional football dynasty. His team was the powerhouse of the NFL during the 1960s—a team driven to near perfection by an intensely competitive, perfectionist leader. Lombardi's image was immortalized in the famous statement "Winning isn't everything, it's the only thing." But did you know that Lombardi never actually said that? Years after his death, his son revealed that his father had been misquoted. What Lombardi actually said was "Winning isn't everything, but striving to win is."

John Wooden was another winner, and so were the UCLA Bruins who played for him. During a 12-year period from 1963 through 1975, his teams won the national collegiate basketball championship ten times. Certainly, to be that successful, Wooden and his Bruins had to be single-mindedly focused on winning games. And yet, at least where Wooden was concerned, this was not the case. In fact, just like Lombardi, he placed an emphasis on the process of *striving for excellence*.

Yes, Lombardi and Wooden were winners. Their won-lost records speak for themselves. But their vision went beyond a preoccupation with winning games. Instead, they demanded that their players dedicate themselves to 100% effort.

The common notion in sports equates success with victory—scoring more points, runs, or goals than the opponent. Yet in a youth sport model the measure of a person's or a team's success goes beyond records and standings. Success is a personal thing and is related to one's own standards and abilities.

Wooden's perspective on success may be the most important reason he deserves the title "Wizard of Westwood." He realized that everyone can be a success because success relates to the effort put into realizing one's personal potential.

The Real Meaning of Winning

In terms of the educational benefits of sport, children can learn from both winning and losing. But for this to occur, winning must be placed in a *healthy* perspective. We have therefore developed a four-part philosophy of winning designed to maximize youth athletes' enjoyment of sport and their chances of achieving the positive outcomes of participation.

1. *Winning isn't everything, nor is it the only thing.* Young athletes can't possibly learn from winning and losing if they think the only objective is to beat their opponents. Does this mean that you should not try to build winning teams? Definitely not! As a form of competition, sport involves a contest between opposing individuals or teams. It would be naive and unrealistic to believe that winning is not an important goal in sports. But it is not the most important objective.

Children should leave your program having enjoyed relating to you and their teammates, feeling better about themselves, having improved their skills, and looking forward to future sport participation. When this happens, something far more valuable has been accomplished than having a winning record or winning a league championship.

2. *Failure is not the same thing as losing.* Athletes should not view losing as a sign of failure or as a threat to their personal value. They should be taught that losing a game is not a reflection of their own self-worth. In other words, when individuals or teams lose a contest it does not mean that they are worth less than if they had won. In fact, some valuable lessons can be learned from losing. Children can learn to persist in the face of obstacles and to support each other even when they do not achieve victory.

3. *Success is not equivalent to winning.* Thus neither success nor failure need depend on the outcome of a contest or on a won-lost record. Winning and losing apply to the outcome of a contest, whereas success and failure do not. How, then, can we define success in sports?

4. *Athletes should be taught that success is found in striving for victory.* The important idea is that *success is related to effort!* The only thing that athletes have complete control over is the amount of effort they

> **Key Principle**
>
> "The only successful youth sports program is the one with the coach who will accept the losing along with the winning, last place in the league along with the first place, and still be able to congratulate his team for their efforts."
>
> Roger Staubach, former Dallas Cowboys quarterback

give. They have only limited control over the outcome that is achieved. If you can impress on your athletes that they are never "losers" if they give maximum effort, you are giving them a priceless gift that will assist them in many of life's tasks. A youth soccer coach had the right idea when he told his team "You kids are always winners when you try your best! But sometimes the other team will score more goals."

When winning is kept in perspective, the child comes first and winning is second. In this case, the most important coaching product is not a won-lost record; it is the quality of the sport experience provided for the athletes.

Youth Sports and the Bigger Picture

I am worried about my son. He seems to have gotten things out of perspective as far as sports are concerned. Although he's only 13 years old, he is convinced that his future lies in college and professional sports. Nothing else seems to matter.

Earlier in this chapter we indicated that athletics can contribute to the personal, social, and physical well-being of youngsters. Sport is an important area in the lives of many children. And for a small number, youth sports are the first phase of a journey that ends in a career in professional athletics.

To strive for high standards of athletic excellence is commendable. But coaches, parents, and athletes alike must realize that the chances of actually becoming a professional are remote. Even if a child appears to be a gifted athlete, the odds are overwhelming. According to Dr. Richard Lapchick, director of the Center for the Study of Sports in Society, the chance of a high-school athlete becoming a professional in any sport is 1 in 12,000.

Key Principle

The stiff odds against a child becoming a college or professional athlete indicate that youth sports should not be treated as a feeder system. Instead the focus should be on personal growth and development.

Given the reality of the situation, a career in professional sports or even participation at the college level is an unrealistic goal for the majority of young athletes. It is therefore important to impress on youngsters that sport is but one part of life for a well-rounded person. It is all too easy for young athletes to harbor fantasies of turning pro and to sacrifice other areas of their development in pursuit of that fabled status and its rewards of fame, money, and glory.

As valuable as atethics can be for developing children, social and academic development, spiritual enrichment, and quality of family life should not suffer. Sports can offer both fun and fulfillment, but there is more to life than sports.

Perhaps the best advice we can give is to encourage children to participate in sports if they wish. But at the same time coaches should help athletes to understand that sport participation is not an end in itself, but a means of achieving various goals. You can teach them to enjoy the process of competition for itself, rather than to focus on such end products as victories and trophies. Neither victory nor defeat should be blown out of proportion, and no coach should permit a child to define his or her self-worth purely on the basis of sport performance. By keeping sports in perspective, you can make them a source of personal growth and enrichment.

Part 2

Becoming a Better Coach

Sport Science and the Youth Coach

Welcome to the world of coaching! You will find that you are far more than "just a coach." You are a teacher, amateur psychologist, substitute parent, and an important role model. Do you feel prepared to fulfill these diverse roles?

As a coach you are probably familiar with sport techniques and strategies. On the other hand, you may not be fully prepared to deal with young athletes who rely on you to provide a worthwhile and enjoyable experience. Each youngster differs in ability and personality and has different reasons for playing a sport. Some hope to be future champions; most simply want to have fun; and others are there because their parents or friends have pressured them into participating. There are even those who wonder what they are doing there. And there you are, trying to meet the needs and expectations of a highly varied group of young personalities. As one experienced coach recalls:

> I'll never forget my first day as a coach. There I was, with a dozen kids looking at me and waiting to be told what to do. I remember thinking 'What do I do now. How did I get myself into this?' I know a lot about sports, but I've never coached kids.

Why Coaches Are Important

Many coaches tend to underestimate the influence they can have on the youngsters who play for them. Children are often able to hide their true feelings, especially in settings where the traditional "strong ath-

Key Principle

A coach can be completely unaware of the influence he or she is having in the life of a child athlete.

lete" image dominates. But in reality, you play a very prominent role in their lives. Your actions and attitudes help to shape their view of the world and of themselves.

Not only do coaches occupy a key position in sports, but their influence can also extend into other areas of children's lives as well. For the many children from single-parent families, coaches may occupy the role of a substitute parent, with enormous potential for a positive impact. One college athlete still remembers her first coach:

> My youth soccer coach was the one person I could talk to. Even though I couldn't really discuss the trouble I was having with my folks, my coach was one person who made me feel that someone cared. I wish I could find her and tell her how much she meant to me.

Should this potential impact on a child's life scare you? Not if you have a genuine concern for youngsters and if you have established for yourself what it is you are attempting to accomplish through coaching. As a coach, you can make an important contribution that, coupled with the contributions of other responsible adults, helps a child on the way to a happy, productive, and well-adjusted life.

The Psychology of Coaching

Much of human interaction consists of attempts to influence the behavior of other people. As a coach, you are trying to influence your athletes in many important ways. One of your most important goals is to create a good learning situation where youngsters can acquire the technical skills needed to succeed as individuals and as a team. Another priority for most coaches is to create a social environment where the participants can relate well to each other and to the coach. This is certainly a key factor in building team cohesion, in making athletes more receptive to your coaching, and in fostering a supportive climate—a setting where athletes can develop teamwork, dedication, mental toughness, and other valued psychological characteristics.

The decisions you make and things you do are attempts to influ-

Key Principle

The psychology of coaching is simply a set of strategies designed to increase your ability to influence others positively.

ence athletes in positive ways. Actually, almost everything you do as a coach can be viewed as attempts to increase certain desired behaviors and to decrease undesirable behaviors.

In the chapters to follow, we will present some psychological principles that you can use to become a more effective coach. Many of the principles will be recognized as things you already do. There is nothing mystical about them. In fact, it is often said that psychology is the application of common sense. The coaching guidelines that we will present make good sense. But more important, research has shown them to be effective ways to increase motivation, morale, enjoyment of the athletic situation, and performance.

> The toughest and most challenging part of coaching is the psychology of getting what you want to teach across to the kids, gaining their respect, and making them feel happy that they know you. When things click on a psychological level, I find that I get much more enjoyment out of coaching.
>
> *A youth wrestling coach*

Positive Versus Negative Approaches to Coaching

There are two basic approaches to influencing the behavior of others. Psychologists refer to these as *positive control* and *aversive control*. Both forms of control are based on the fact that behavior is strongly influenced by the consequences it produces. Responses that lead to positive or desired outcomes are strengthened, and their likelihood of occurring in the future is increased. On the other hand, behaviors that result in undesirable or unpleasant consequences are less likely to be repeated. Positive and aversive control underlie what we have labeled the *positive approach* and the *negative approach* to coaching.

The positive approach is designed to strengthen desired behaviors by motivating athletes to perform them and by rewarding the athletes when they do. On the other hand, the negative approach involves attempts to eliminate unwanted behaviors through punishment and criticism. The motivating factor in this approach is fear. Research studies indicate that most coaches use a combination of positive and aversive control.

In our society, aversive control through punishment is perhaps the most widespread means of controlling behavior. Our entire system of laws is backed up by threats of punishment. Similarly, fear of failure is one means of promoting school achievement, social development, and other desired behaviors. The reason punishment is the glue that holds so much of our society's fabric together is that for the most part it *seems* to work. It is the fastest way to bring behavior under control. In sports, punishment finds its expression in the negative approach to coaching.

Key Principle
The negative approach to coaching is characterized by the use of punishment and criticism to eliminate mistakes. It operates through the creation of fear.

Frequently in sports we hear the statement "The team that makes the fewest mistakes will win." And this is usually the case. Many coaches therefore develop coaching tactics oriented toward eliminating mistakes. The seemingly obvious approach is to use aversive control. To get rid of mistakes, coaches simply punish athletes when they make them. The assumption is that if they make athletes frightened enough of making mistakes, they are more likely to perform well.

We do not have to look far to find examples of highly successful coaches who are "screamers" and whose teams seem to perform like well-oiled machines. Other less-experienced coaches may conclude that this is the most effective way to train athletes. They adopt this part of the successful coaches' behavior, perhaps to the exclusion of other teaching techniques that probably are the true keys to the success of the "screamers."

Key Principle
Punitive coaching behaviors have many undesirable side effects that can actually interfere with what a coach is trying to accomplish. It is the fastest way to instill fear of failure and to create resistance and hostility.

There is evidence that punishment and criticism can decrease unwanted behaviors. But the evidence is equally strong that punishment has certain undesirable side effects. These can actually interfere with what a coach is trying to accomplish. First and foremost, punishment works by creating fear.

Using too much punishment promotes the development of fear of failure. This is undoubtedly the least desirable form of athletic motivation. If it becomes the primary motive for athletic performance, it not only decreases enjoyment of the activity but also increases the likelihood of failure.

The athlete with a high fear of failure is motivated, not by a positive desire to achieve and enjoy "the thrill of victory," but by fear of "the agony of defeat." Athletic competition is transformed from a challenge into a threat. Because high anxiety disrupts motor performance and interferes with thinking, the high-fear-of-failure athlete is prone to "choke" under pressure. This is because concentration is more on the feared consequences of mistakes than what positively needs to be done. Studies have shown that athletes who have a high fear of failure not only perform more poorly in competition but also are at a greater risk for injury, enjoy the sport experience less, and are more likely to drop out of sports.

Punishment has other potential side effects that most coaches want to avoid. A predominance of aversive control makes for an unpleasant teaching situation. It arouses resentment and hostility, which may be masked by the power difference that exists between coach and athlete. It may produce a kind of cohesion among athletes based on their mutual dislike for the coach. It is even possible that athletes may consciously or subconsciously act in ways that sabotage what the coach is trying to accomplish. Moreover, coaches occupy a role that is admired by athletes, and they should not overlook their importance as models for young people who are developing socially. The abusive "screamer" is certainly not exhibiting the kinds of behaviors that will contribute to the personal growth of athletes who imitate the coach.

Fortunately there is an alternative to the negative approach. The positive approach accomplishes everything that aversive control does, and much more, without the harmful side effects. The positive approach is aimed at strengthening desired behaviors through the use of encourage-

Key Principle

The positive approach to coaching is designed to increase desirable behaviors and to create positive motivation rather than fear of failing. It has none of the negative side effects of the negative approach.

ment, positive reinforcement, and technical instruction. From this point of view, the best way to eliminate mistakes is not to try to stamp them out with punishment, but rather to strengthen the *correct* behaviors. The motivational force at work is a positive desire to achieve rather than a negative fear of failure. The positive approach, through its emphasis on improving rather than on "not screwing up," fosters a more desirable learning environment and tends to promote more positive relationships among coaches and athletes. Prominent coaches like Jimmy Johnson recognize and practice the power of the positive approach:

> I try never to plant a negative seed. I try to make every comment a positive comment. There's a lot of scientific evidence to support positive management.

Scientific Evidence Supports the Positive Approach

A qualified coach must understand more than the mechanics of sports. This individual must be able to create a healthy psychological environment for young athletes—an environment that promotes athletic, personal, and social development. Methods for doing so have been developed within a program known as Coach Effectiveness Training™ (CET).

Key Principle
Coach Effectiveness Training is based on scientific studies of coaching behaviors and their effects on young athletes.

CET is based on scientific evidence derived from 20 years of research at the University of Washington. In our Youth Sport Enrichment Project, we studied coaching behaviors and their effects on young athletes. First we determined how specific coaching behaviors were related to athletes' attitudes toward their coach, teammates, and other aspects of their sport participation. We also studied how characteristics of the children, such as their age and level of self-esteem, affected their responses to specific coaching styles.

We then used the research results to develop a set of coaching guidelines that form the core of CET. To test the effectiveness of the coach training program, we carried out a series of program evaluation studies. In these studies, one group of coaches participated in a two-

and-a-half hour CET workshop, serving as an experimental group. They were compared with other coaches who did not receive any special training (that is, a control group). We studied how the two groups of coaches behaved during practices and games, and we measured the sport-related attitudes and several personality factors in the youngsters who played for them.

We have focused on five important outcome questions in our program evaluation studies:

- Does the CET program affect the behaviors of coaches in a manner consistent with the coaching guidelines?

- Does the program favorably affect children's reactions to their athletic experience and their liking for coaches and teammates?

- Does playing for a CET coach result in an increase in athletes' self-esteem?

- Does CET training help reduce athletes' performance anxiety (fear of failure)?

- Do positive changes in the first four outcomes increase the likelihood that young athletes will choose to remain in a sport program rather than dropping out?

The results of the program evaluation studies have been very encouraging. The answer to all five of the outcome questions was a resounding YES!

Coaches exposed to CET differed in both observed behaviors and in athlete-perceived behaviors in a manner consistent with the CET coaching guidelines. Observations during practices and games showed that CET coaches were more reinforcing, more encouraging, gave more technical instruction, and were less punitive and controlling than were control-group coaches. The athletes reported experiencing these same differences in coaching styles. In turn, youngsters who played for the CET coaches indicated that they liked their

Key Principle

Coach Effectiveness Training favorably affects liking for the coach, teammates, and the sport experience. It also increases children's self-esteem, reduces performance anxiety, and counteracts dropout.

coach and teammates more, and that they had more fun. On psychological tests they also demonstrated significant increases in self-esteem and significant decreases in performance anxiety over the course of the season. Finally, a one-year followup study showed a dropout rate of 26% among children who played for untrained coaches, a figure that is quite consistent with previous reports of attrition in youth sports. In contrast, only 5% of the children who had played for CET-trained coaches failed to return to the program the next season.[1]

In summary, CET has proven to be an effective program that alters coaching behaviors in a desirable fashion and thereby has positive effects on the children who play for trained coaches. All five classes of outcome variables—coaching behaviors, children's attitudes, self-esteem, performance anxiety, and drop out—have been significantly and positively influenced by the CET program.

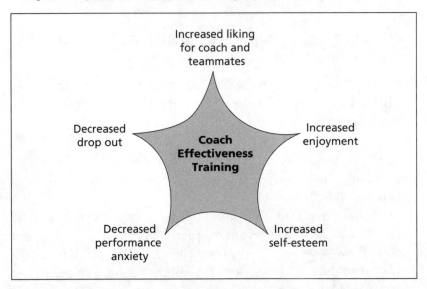

Just as the CET coaches did, you can use the coaching guidelines to improve the quality of your athletes' sport experience. The challenge is not so much in learning the principles but in adapting them to your own coaching style. This requires dedication on your part. However, the favorable outcomes will be well worth the extra effort!

[1] Citations for the scientific studies of CET are included in the reference section at the end of the book.

Increasing Your Coaching Effectiveness

4

W e have seen that coaches who received Coach Effectiveness Training were able to create a positive sport environment that had beneficial effects on their young athletes. In interviewing these coaches, it was also clear that they, like their athletes, enjoyed their experience. What did the CET coaches do that made such a difference?

This chapter presents the principles that underlie a positive approach to effective coach-athlete interaction. More specifically, we will examine a series of behavioral guidelines (coaching "do's and don'ts") that form the foundation of a relationship-oriented style of coaching. These behavioral guidelines are placed in a goal context of increasing positive coach-athlete and athlete-athlete interaction, developing team cohesion, and developing in athletes a positive desire to achieve rather than a fear of failure.

This relationship-oriented style complements the healthy philosophy of winning presented in Chapter 2—giving total effort in striving for excellence. If young athletes are well trained, give maximum effort, and have a positive motivation to achieve rather than a performance-disrupting fear of failure, winning takes care of itself within the limits of their abilities. They also are more likely to develop their athletic potential in an enjoyable rather than stressful sport environment.

Using the Power of Reinforcement

Our emphasis on influencing athletes' behavior in a desirable way involves the process of learning. It is well known that people tend to

Key Principle

The most effective way to build and strengthen desirable behaviors is to use your "reinforcement power."

repeat behaviors that produce pleasant outcomes. In this context, *reinforcement* refers to any event occurring after a behavior that increases the likelihood that the behavior will occur again in the future. (It is similar to the more familiar concept of *reward*, but psychologists prefer the term *reinforcement* because what is "rewarding" for one person may not be a reward for another.) The cornerstone of the positive approach is the skilled use of reinforcement to increase athletic motivation and to strengthen desired behaviors. Indeed, positive reinforcement is the most powerful way to develop and strengthen desired behaviors in athletes. As our CET outcome studies showed, it also produces an enjoyable and growth-promoting sport environment.

Choosing a reinforcer is not usually difficult. But in some cases your creativity and sensitivity to the needs of individual athletes might be tested. Potential reinforcers include social behaviors such as verbal praise, nonverbal signs such as smiles or applause, and physical contact such as a pat on the back. They also include the opportunity to engage in certain activities (such as extra batting practice) or to play with a particular piece of equipment.

Key Principle

The best way to find an effective reinforcer is to get to know each athlete's likes and dislikes. In this area it is "different strokes for different folks."

Social reinforcers are most frequently employed in athletics. But even here you must decide what is most likely to be effective with each athlete. One athlete might find praise given in the presence of others highly reinforcing, whereas another might find it embarassing.

In some instances you may elect to praise an entire unit or group of athletes. At other times, reinforcement may be directed at one athlete. If at all possible, it is a good idea to use a variety of reinforcers and vary what you say and do so that you don't begin to sound like a broken record. In the final analysis, the acid test of your choice of reinforcer is whether it affects behavior in the desired manner.

Here are some principles for the effective use of your "reinforcement power."

1. *Be liberal with reinforcement.* In our research, the single most important difference between coaches to whom athletes responded most favorably and those they evaluated least favorably was the frequency with which coaches reinforced desirable behaviors. You can increase the effectiveness of verbal reinforcement by combining it with a specific description of the desirable behavior that the athlete just performed. For example, you might say, "Way to go, Chris! You kept your head in there on the follow-through." In this way, you combine the power of the reinforcement with an instructional reminder of what the athlete should do. It also cues the athlete about what to concentrate on.

Reinforcement should not be restricted to the learning and performance of sport skills. Rather, it should also be liberally applied to strengthen desirable psychosocial behaviors, such as teamwork, leadership, and sportsmanship. Look for positive things, reinforce them, and you will see them increase. Reinforce the little things that others might not notice. We are not promoting a sickening sweet approach with which there is a danger of being phony and losing credibility. When sincerely given, reinforcement does not spoil youngsters; it gives them something to strive for. Remember, whether athletes show it or not, the reinforcement you give them helps strengthen the good feelings they have about themselves.

2. *Have realistic expectations and consistently reinforce achievement.* Gear your expectations to individual ability levels. For some athletes, merely running up and down the field or court without tripping is a significant accomplishment worthy of praise. For those who are more skilled, set your expectations at appropriately higher levels.

In many instances, complex skills can be broken down into their component sub-

Key Principle

Successful coaching requires skillful use of reinforcement. Start reinforcing what each athlete is capable of doing, and gradually require more as skills are refined.

skills. You can then concentrate on one of these subskills at a time until it is mastered. For example, a football coach might choose to concentrate entirely on the pattern run by a pass receiver with no concern about whether the pass is completed. This is where your knowledge of the sport and of the mastery levels of your individual athletes is crucial. Athletes can enjoy lots of support and reinforcement long before they have completely mastered the entire skill if you are attentive to their instructional needs and progress.

Start with what the athlete is currently capable of doing and then gradually require more and more of the athlete before reinforcement is given. It is important that the shift in demands be realistic and that the steps be small enough so that the athlete can master them and be reinforced. Used correctly, progressive reinforcement is one of the most powerful of all the positive control techniques.

Once skills are well learned, gradually shift your reinforcement to a partial schedule. This means that some correct responses are reinforced, and some are not. Research has shown that behaviors reinforced on partial schedules persist much longer in the absence of reinforcement than do actions that have been reinforced only on a continuous schedule. As casino owners are well aware, people will put a great many coins into slot machines, which operate on partial schedules. In contrast, they are unlikely to persist long in putting coins into soft drink machines that do not deliver. Thus the key is to start with continuous reinforcement until the skill is mastered. Then shift gradually to partial reinforcement to maintain a high level of motivation and performance.

3. *Give reinforcement for desirable behavior as soon as it occurs.* The timing of reinforcement is another important consideration. Other things being equal, the sooner reinforcement occurs after a response the stronger are its effects. Whenever possible, try to reinforce a desired behavior as soon as it occurs. If this is not possible, try to find an opportunity to praise the athlete later on.

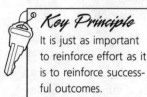

Key Principle
It is just as important to reinforce effort as it is to reinforce successful outcomes.

4. *Reinforce effort as much as results.* This guideline has direct relevance to developing a healthy philosophy of winning.

To put this philosophy into practice, tell your athletes that their efforts are valued and appreciated, and back up your words with action (reinforcement). Athletes' efforts should not be ignored.

As a coach, you have a right to demand total effort. This may be the most important thing for you to reinforce. We stated in Chapter 2 that athletes have complete control over how much effort they make, but they have only limited control over the outcome of their efforts. By looking for and reinforcing athletes' efforts you can encourage them to continue or increase their output.

A Positive Approach to Mistakes

Many athletes are motivated to achieve because of a positive desire to succeed. They appear to welcome, and peak, under pressure. Unfortunately many others are motivated primarily by fear of failure, and consequently they dread critical situations and the possibility of failure and disapproval. Fear of failure is an athlete's worst enemy. It can harm performance, and it reduces the enjoyment of competing. The way you react to athletes' mistakes plays a major role in either creating or combating fear of failure.

Key Principle

If you manage things right, mistakes can be golden opportunities to improve performance, for they provide the feedback that is needed to make adjustments.

A typical attitude about mistakes is that they are totally bad and must be avoided at all costs. Rather than focusing on the negative aspects of mistakes, recognize that they are not only unavoidable but they also have a positive side. John Wooden referred to mistakes as the "stepping stones to achievement." They provide information that is needed to improve performance. By communicating this concept to athletes in word and action, you can help them accept and learn from their mistakes.

In addition, remember that what you say and do has an important effect on athletes. Thus deal honestly and openly with your own mistakes. When you have the confidence and courage to admit that you made a mistake, you provide a valuable role model. Such a model is important for developing a sense of tolerance for human error and for reducing fear of failure. Remember, the positive approach is designed to create a positive motive to achieve rather than a fear of failure. This lesson was not lost on Coach John Wooden:

> You must know quite well that you are not perfect, that you're going to make mistakes. But you must not be afraid of making mistakes or you won't do anything, and that's the greatest mistake of all. We must have initiative and act and know that we're going to fail at times, for failure will only make us stronger if we accept it properly.

Here are some practical guidelines for reacting to mistakes.

1. *Give encouragement immediately after a mistake.* Athletes know when they made a poor play and often feel embarrassed about it. This is the time they are in most need of your encouragement and support.

2. *If an athlete knows how to correct the mistake, encouragement alone is sufficient.* Telling athletes what they already know may be more irritating than helpful. Don't overload athletes with unnecessary input. If you are not sure whether the athlete knows how to correct the mistake, ask the athlete for confirmation.

3. *When appropriate, give corrective instruction after a mistake, but always do so in an encouraging and positive way.* In line with the positive approach, mistakes can be excellent opportunities to provide technical instruction. There are three keys to giving such instruction:

- Know *what* to do—the technical aspects of correcting performance.
- Know *how* to do it—the teaching-learning approach.
- Know *when* to do it—timing.

Most athletes respond best to immediate correction, and instruction is particularly meaningful at that time. However, some athletes respond much better to instruction if you wait for some time after the mistake. Because of individual differences, such athletes are more receptive to your instruction when it is given later.

When correcting mistakes, a three-part teaching approach which we call "the positive sandwich" is recommended. In the following example, a football player has dropped a pass because he took his eyes off the ball:

- *Start with a compliment;* find something the athlete did correctly ("Way to hustle. You really ran a good pattern!"). This is intended to reinforce a desirable behavior and create an open attitude on the part of the athlete.

> **Key Principle**
>
> In giving corrective instruction, don't emphasize the bad effects of the mistake. Instead, point out the good things that will happen if the athlete follows your instruction.

- *Give the future-oriented instruction* ("If you follow the ball all the way into your hands, you'll catch those just like a pro does.") Emphasize the desired *future* outcome rather than the negative one that just occurred.

- *End with another positive statement* ("Hang in there. You're going to get even better if you work at it.") This "positive sandwich" approach (two positive communications wrapped around the instruction) is designed to make the athlete positively self-motivated to perform correctly rather than negatively motivated to avoid failure and disapproval.

4. *Don't punish when things go wrong.* Punishment is any consequence that decreases the future occurrence of a behavior. Punishment can be administered in either of two forms: (a) by doing something aversive, such as verbal abuse, or (b) by taking something that is valued away from the athlete, or more technically, by removing positive reinforcers that are usually available, such as privileges, social interactions, or possessions. With respect to the first form, punishment is not just yelling at athletes. It can be any form of disapproval, tone of voice, or action. Constant use of such punishment leads to resentment of the coach and is a probable factor contributing to lack of enjoyment and athletic dropout.

5. *Don't give corrective instruction in a hostile or punitive way.* Although a coach may have good intentions in giving instruction, this kind of negative communication is more likely to increase frustration and create resentment than to improve performance.

Does this mean that you should avoid all criticism and punishment? Certainly not! Sometimes, these behaviors are necessary for instructional or disciplinary purposes. But they should be used sparingly. If you feel that you must use punishment, do it only as a last resort, and do it in such a way that it's clear that you dislike the behavior, not the person. The negative approach should never be the primary approach to athletes. As coach Jimmy Johnson notes, "We rely 90% on positive reinforcement. But when we do use punishment, it really makes an impact."

Although abusive coaches may enjoy success and may even be admired by some of their athletes, they run the risk of losing other athletes who could contribute to the team's success and who could profit personally from an athletic experience. Coaches who succeed through the use of punishment and intimidation usually do so because (a) they are also able to communicate caring for their athletes as people, so that the abuse is not "taken personally," (b) they have very talented athletes, and/or (c) they are such skilled teachers and strategists that these abilities override their negative behaviors. In other words, such coaches win *in spite of*, not because of, the negative approach.

Maintaining Order and Discipline

Problems of athlete misbehavior during practices and contests (games, matches, meets) can indeed become serious. In dealing effectively with this, recognize that youngsters want clearly defined limits and structure. They do not like unpredictability and inconsistency. On the other hand, they do not like it when you play the role of a policeman or enforcer. Thus the objective is to structure the situation so that you can teach discipline without having to constantly read the riot act to keep things under control. The following statements are guidelines to maintaining order and discipline.

Key Principle

Teaching self-discipline is an important youth sport objective. But it need not be based on punitive control; the positive approach can be applied here as well.

1. *Maintain order by establishing clear expectations and a "team rule" concept.*

2. *Involve athletes in forming behavioral guidelines and work to build team unity in achieving them.*

3. *Strive to achieve a balance between freedom and structure.*

These guidelines promote a cooperative approach to leadership in that athletes are given a share of the responsibility for determining their own governance. The rationale for this approach is that people are more willing to live by rules (a) when they have a hand in forming them, and (b) when they have made a public commitment to follow them. There is considerable research support for this rationale in psychology.

Team rules should be developed early in the season. In helping athletes to share responsibility for forming rules, use the following procedures:

- Explain why team rules are necessary (they keep things organized and efficient, thereby increasing the chances of achieving individual and team objectives).

- Explain why the team rules should be something that they can agree on as a group (the rules will be *their* rules, and it will be *their* responsibility to follow them).

- Solicit suggestions and ideas, and listen to what athletes say to show that their ideas and feelings are valued.

- Incorporate athletes' input into a reasonable set of rules. Rules should provide structure and yet not be too rigid. Examples of such rules might be: (a) be prepared and focused during practice and competition, (b) give maximum effort at all times, and (c) treat others as you want to be treated.

- Discuss the kinds of penalties that you will use for breaking team rules. Here again, athletes should participate in determining the consequences that will follow rule violations.

The advantage of this approach is that it places the responsibility where it belongs—on the athletes themselves. In this way, team discipline can help develop self-discipline. Then, when someone breaks a team rule, it is not the individual versus your rules, but the breaking of their own rules. This system was used by former North Carolina basketball coach Dean Smith: "We have very few rules on our basketball team, and all of the rules are made by our players. The coaching staff is pledged to uphold and enforce them."

4. *Emphasize that during a contest all members of the team are part of the contest, even those on the bench.* This rule can play an important role in building team cohesion and mutual support among teammates.

5. *Use reinforcement to strengthen team participation and unity.* By strengthening desirable behaviors, you can help prevent misbehaviors from occurring. In other words, you can prevent misbehaviors by using the positive approach to strengthen their opposites. Similarly, instances of teamwork and of athletes' support and encouragement of each other should be acknowledged and reinforced whenever possible. This not only strengthens these desirable behaviors, but also creates an atmosphere in which you yourself are serving as a positive model by supporting them.

Dealing with Team Rule Violations

When you have team rules, you can expect that they will be broken from time to time. As youngsters establish independence and personal identity, part of the process involves testing the limits imposed by adult authority figures—people like you! Because this is a very natural process in development, you should not feel persecuted or take it too personally. It happens with all youth coaches (as well as high school, college, and professional coaches) from time to time, and therefore these recommendations for dealing with team rules are presented.

Key Principle
Don't take it personally when rules are violated; it's a natural part of establishing independence. There are productive ways of dealing with such violations.

1. *Allow the athlete to explain his/her actions.* There may be a reasonable cause for the athlete's behavior, and lines of communication should be kept open.

2. *Be consistent and impartial.* In other words, avoid showing favoritism by treating *all* athletes—the stars and the subs—equally and fairly. Fairness builds respect.

3. *Don't express anger and a punitive attitude.* And, of course, never take action for the purpose of retaliating.

4. *Don't lecture or embarrass the athlete.* It simply is neither necessary nor beneficial.

5. *Focus on the fact that a team policy has been broken, placing the responsibility on the athlete.* This should be done without degrading the individual or making the athlete feel "in the dog house." Remind the athlete that a rule was violated that the athlete agreed to follow, and because of that a penalty must be paid. This focuses the responsibility where it belongs—on the athlete—and helps build a sense of personal accountability.

6. *When giving penalties, it is best to deprive athletes of something they value.* For example, participation can be temporarily suspended by having the player sit off to the side ("time out" or "penalty box"). Taking away playing time or a starting position are also effective penalties.

7. *Don't use physical measures that could become aversive by being used to punish (running laps, doing push-ups).* It is not educationally sound to have beneficial physical activities become unpleasant because they have been used as punishment.

Building Team Unity and Cohesion

One of the greatest pleasures of sport participation comes from the comaraderie that develops between coaches and athletes and among teammates. Research has also shown that cohesive and mutually supportive teams tend to be more successful. Thus one goal of the positive approach is to produce team unity and cohesion in which mutual respect and support are the norm. Our research revealed that CET coaches were able to create a socially supportive environment by using the guidelines and principles presented below.

> *Key Principle*
>
> The positive approach is a proven way to develop team cohesion. This is done by modeling and reinforcing mutually supportive behaviors.

1. *Set a good example of behavior.* Children learn a great deal by watching and imitating others. Imitation (or modeling) is an important form of learning for children. Most athletes will have a high regard for you, and consequently they are likely to copy your behaviors and deal with sport situations in similar ways. Athletes probably learn as much from what you do as from what you say! Because of this, it is important that you portray a role model worthy of respect from athletes, officials, parents, and other coaches as well. If you exhibit respect and consideration for your athletes, they are more likely to do likewise. You can also promote and strengthen cohesion in the following ways.

2. *Encourage effort, don't demand results.* This is another guideline that applies to the healthy philosophy of winning presented in Chapter 2. Most young athletes are already motivated to develop their skills and play well. By appropriate use of encouragement, you can help to increase their natural enthusiasm. If, however, youngsters are encouraged to strive for unrealistic standards of achievement, they may feel like failures when they do not reach the goals. Therefore it is important to base your encouragement on reasonable expectations. Again, emphasizing effort rather than outcome can help avoid problems. This concept is illustrated in the words of John Wooden:

> You cannot find a player who ever played for me at UCLA who can tell you that he ever heard me mention "winning" a basketball game. He might say I inferred a little here and there, but I never mentioned winning. Yet the last thing that I told my players, just prior to tipoff, before we would go on the floor was, "When the game is over, I want your head up—and I know of only one way for your head to be up—and that's for you to know that you did your best . . . This means to do the best you can do. That's the best; no one can do more . . . You made that effort.

3. *In giving encouragement, be selective so that it is meaningful.* In other words, be supportive without acting like a cheerleader.

4. *Never give encouragement or instruction in a sarcastic or degrading manner.* For example, "Come on gang, we're only down 37–1. Let's really come back and make it 37–2!" Even if you do not intend the sarcasm to be harmful, youngsters sometimes do not understand the meaning of this type of communication. They may think that you are

amusing others at their expense, which can result in irritation or frustration.

5. *Encourage athletes to be supportive of each other, and reinforce them when they do so.* Encouragement can become contagious and contribute to building team cohesion. Communicate the enthusiasm you feel, which then carries over to your athletes. The best way to do this is by (a) presenting an enthusiastic coaching model, and (b) reinforcing athlete behaviors that promote team unity.

Teaching Sport Skills Effectively

Young athletes expect you to help them satisfy their desire to become as skilled as possible. Therefore, you must establish your teaching role as early as possible. In doing this, emphasize the pleasure and learning aspects of sport, and let your athletes know that a primary coaching goal is to help them develop their athletic potential.

During each practice or contest, be sure that every youngster gets recognized at least once. Athletes who usually get the most recognition are (a) stars, or (b) those who are causing problems. Average athletes need attention too! A good technique is to occasionally keep a count of how often you talk with each athlete to make sure that your personal contact is being appropriately distributed.

> **Key Principle**
>
> "When we have conferences with our Nebraska players, we always start out by discussing what their strengths are. Everyone needs to hear this. Then we tell them what they need to improve on, with specific instructions on how they can improve."
> Tom Osborne, former University of Nebraska football coach

1. *Always give instructions positively.* Emphasize the good things that will happen if athletes do it right rather than focusing totally on the negative things that will occur if they do not. As stated earlier, this approach motivates athletes to make desirable things happen rather than building fear of making mistakes.

2. *When giving instructions, be clear and concise.* Young athletes have a short attention span. In addition, they may not be able to understand the technical aspects of performance in great detail. Therefore, provide

simple yet accurate teaching cues, using as little verbal explanation as possible.

3. *Show athletes the correct technique.* Demonstrate or model skills being taught. If you cannot perform the skill correctly, use accomplished athletes for demonstration purposes. A proper teaching sequence includes the following:

- Introduce a skill with a demonstration.

- Provide an accurate, but brief verbal explanation.

- Have athletes actively practice the skill.

- Give constructive feedback, encouragement, and individual instruction as needed.

Because of the way in which children respond to teaching efforts, a Chinese proverb applies: "I hear and I forget. I see and I remember. I do and I understand."

4. *Be patient and don't expect or demand more than maximum effort.* Acquisition of sport skills does not occur overnight. The gradual learning process is characterized by periods of improvement alternated with times in which no progress occurs regardless of the effort expended. Not only must you be persistent, but athletes must be convinced to stick to it and continue to give their best effort.

When an athlete has had a poor practice or a rough game, the youngster should not go home feeling badly. He or she should get some kind of support from you—a pat on the back, a kind word ("Hey, we're going to work that out. I know what you're going through, but everyone has days like that sometimes."). Athletes should not leave feeling cut off from you or feeling like a "loser."

5. *Reinforce effort and progress.* Again, the foundation of the positive approach is generous reinforcement for effort as well as desirable performance and psychosocial behavior.

Communication and Self-Awareness

As a coach you are giving a great deal of time and energy to provide a worthwhile life experience for children. By putting to use the basic principles described above, you can increase the positive impact you

> **Key Principle**
> Communication skills and self-awareness of your own leadership behaviors are keys to coaching effectiveness.

have on young people's lives. A complete understanding of the coaching guidelines is essential for their effective use. In addition, communication skills and self-awareness are important for successful application of the guidelines.

Communicating Effectively

Everything we do communicates something to others. Because of this, develop the habit of asking yourself (and, at times, your athletes) how your actions are being interpreted. You can then evaluate whether you are communicating what you intend to.

Effective communication is a two-way street. By keeping the lines of interaction open, you can be more aware of opportunities to have a positive impact on athletes. Fostering two-way communication does not mean that athletes are free to be disrespectful toward you. Rather

> **Key Principle**
> Constantly ask yourself what has been communicated to athletes and whether the communication is effective.

it invites athletes to express their views (both positive and negative) with the assurance that they will be heard by you. Furthermore, by presenting a model of an attentive listener, you can hope to improve the listening skills of your athletes.

Effective communication also requires that you view a team as a group of individuals and respond to these individuals accordingly. For example, a youngster who has low self-confidence may be crushed (or positively affected) by something that has no impact whatever on an athlete with high self-esteem. By improving your sensitivity to the individual needs of athletes, you can be more successful. The ability to "read" athletes and respond to their needs is characteristic of effective coaches at all levels.

Increasing Self-Awareness

An important part of self-awareness is insight into how we behave and come across to others—knowing what we do and how others perceive what we do. One of the striking findings from our research was that coaches had very limited awareness of how often they behaved in various ways. Fortunately, awareness is something that can be increased.

Two awareness-enhancing techniques are recommended, namely, behavioral feedback and self-monitoring.

Key Principle
Awareness of one's own behavior is central to becoming more effective, and such awareness can be increased through feedback and self-monitoring.

Behavioral feedback. Try to develop procedures that will allow you to obtain feedback from your assistants. In other words, work with assistant coaches as a team and share descriptions of each others' behaviors. You can then discuss alternate ways of dealing with problem situations and athletes and prepare yourself for handling similar situations in the future. Obviously this requires an open relationship between coaches, a willingness to exchange feedback that may not always be positive, and a sincere desire to improve the way you relate to athletes. Finally, at times you may wish to discuss situations with your athletes to obtain feedback from them. This will show your athletes that you are interested in their reactions and are motivated to provide the best possible experience for them.

Self-monitoring. Self-monitoring (observing and recording one's own behavior) involves taking some time after practices and/or contests to evaluate your behaviors and actions. When going through this self-analysis, ask yourself what you did relative to the suggested behaviors in the coaching guidelines. To assist you in this procedure, a brief form is presented (*at the top of the next page*) for self-monitoring of desirable coaching behaviors.

Summary of Coaching Guidelines

Reactings to Player Behaviors and Game Situations

1. *Good plays.*

   Do: Reinforce! Do so immediately. Let the athletes know that you appreciate and value their efforts, and reinforce effort as much as you do results. Look for positive things, reinforce them, and you will see them increase. Remember, whether the children show it or not, the positive things you say and do stick with them.

   Don't: Take their efforts for granted.

Coach Self-Report Form

Complete this form as soon as possible after a practice or contest. Not only think about what you did, but also consider the kinds of situations in which the actions occurred and the kinds of athletes who were involved.

1. Approximately what percent of the time they occurred did you respond to good plays with REINFORCEMENT? _____

2. Approximately what percent of the times they occurred did you respond to mistakes with each of the following communications? _____

    A. **Encouragement** only _____

    B. **Corrective Instruction** given in an encouraging manner _____

    (Sum of A plus B should not exceed 100%)

3. About how many times did you reinforce athletes for effort, complying with team rules, encouraging teammates, showing team spirit, and other behaviors? _____

4. Is there anything you might do differently if you had a chance to coach this practice or contest again? If so, briefly explain.

_____

_____

_____

_____

_____

---

2. *Mistakes, screw-ups, boneheaded plays, and all the things the pros seldom do.*

Do: Encourage immediately after mistakes. That's when the child needs encouragement most. Also, give corrective instruction on how to do it right, but always do so in an encouraging manner. Do this by emphasizing not the bad things that just happened, but the good things that will happen if the child follows your instruction (the *why* of it). This will make the athlete positively self-motivated to correct the mistakes rather than negatively motivated to avoid failure and your disapproval.

Don't: Punish when things are going wrong. Punishment isn't just yelling at children; it can be tone of voice, action, any indication of disapproval. Kids respond much better to a positive approach. Fear of failure is reduced if you work to reduce fear of punishment.

3. *Misbehaviors, lack of attention.*

Do: Maintain order by establishing clear expectations. Emphasize that during a contest all members of the team are part of the activity, even those on the bench. Use reinforcement to strengthen team participation. In other words, try to prevent misbehaviors by using the positive approach to strengthen their opposites.

Don't: Get into the position of having to constantly nag or threaten the athletes in order to prevent chaos. Don't be a drill sergeant. If a child refuses to cooperate, quietly remove him or her from the bench for a period of time. Don't use physical measures, such as running laps. The idea here is that if you establish clear behavioral guidelines early and work to build team spirit in achieving them, you can avoid having to repeatedly keep control. Remember, youngsters want clear guidelines and expectations, but they don't want to be regimented. Try to achieve a healthy balance.

Getting Positive Things to Happen and Creating a Good Learning Atmosphere

Do: Give instruction. Establish your role as a teacher. Try to structure participation as a learning experience in which you are going to help the children develop their abilities. Always give instruction in a positive fashion. Satisfy your athletes' desire to become the best they can be. Give instruction in a clear, concise manner and, if possible, demonstrate how to do it.

Do: Give encouragement. Encourage effort, don't demand results. Use it selectively so that it is meaningful. Be supportive without acting like a cheerleader.

Do: Concentrate on the activity. Be "in the game" with the athletes. Set a good example for team unity.

Don't: Give either instruction or encouragement in a sarcastic or degrading manner. Make a point, then leave it. Don't let "encouragement" become irritating to the athletes.

Part 3

Performance Enhancement for Young Athletes

Systematic Goal Setting to Increase Motivation and Performance

Success in sports, as in any other achievement arena, depends on both skill and motivation. Skill and motivation are intimately related to one another. Athletes who are not motivated to develop their skills will probably not achieve their potential, and inadequate skills will not allow athletes to achieve their goals.

Motivation involves striving for particular goals. Thus success as an athlete, as a coach, and as a team depends in large part on goal setting. Coaches must have goals. Teams must have goals. Individual athletes must have real, vivid, living goals. Goals help to keep everyone on target. Goals commit athletes and coaches to the work, time, pain, and whatever else is part of the price of achieving success. Transforming potential into performance involves setting and attaining goals.

Coaches at all competitive levels are finding that specific goal-setting programs can have dramatic positive effects on both motivation and skill development. Their experiences are mirrored in the results of more than 100 scientific studies of goal-setting programs in business and industry. In over 90% of these studies, measurable increases in performance resulted when goal-setting procedures were introduced. Psychologists have learned a great deal about how to design and carry out effective goal-setting programs. By making use of these principles, you can increase motiva-

Key Principle

Research in many settings, including athletics, has shown that systematic goal setting is one of the most powerful performance enhancement techniques.

tion, performance, and the amount of fun and enjoyment your athletes experience.

How Goal Setting Affects Young Athletes

There are many reasons why goal setting improves performance.

- *Goal setting focuses and directs the athlete's activities.* Goals direct the athlete's attention and action to important aspects of the task. For example, a basketball player who sets a goal of increasing her free-throw shooting percentage to 70% will concentrate on shooting free throws during practice rather than taking many different kinds of shots.

- *Goals help athletes mobilize effort.* Returning to our basketball player, by setting this specific goal, she will likely exhibit greater effort and commitment in attempting to achieve this objective.

> ### Key Principle
> Goal setting operates by directing and mobilizing effort, increasing commitment and persistence, and helping people find new and more effective strategies.

- *Goals not only increase immediate effort but also increase persistence.* As a case in point, the boredom of a long season is offset and persistence is increased when a golfer sets a number of short term goals throughout the year.

- *Athletes develop and use new strategies for improving performance.* For example, a batter may change the mechanics of his swing in order to achieve a goal of hitting a certain percentage of line drives. Thus setting and trying to attain specific goals may help to increase motivation, commitment, and performance.

Keys to Effective Goal Setting

Not all goal-setting procedures are created equal. Some approaches to goal setting are more effective than others. Research on the effectiveness of various types of goal-setting strategies suggests several practical guidelines.

1. *Set specific goals in terms that can be measured.* Specific goals are more effective in improving performance than are general "do your best" goals or no goals at all. Telling an athlete to "do as well as you can" does not make clear exactly what the person is to do. Therefore it is essential that, in the athletic environment, goals be expressed in terms of specific measurable behaviors. Thus setting goals in terms of specific free-throw shooting percentages or number of turnovers is far more effective than encouraging players to "improve your free throw shooting" or "handle the ball better."

2. *Set difficult but realistic goals.* Difficult or challenging goals produce better performance than moderate or easy goals. The higher the goal, the higher the performance, as long as the goal does not exceed what the athlete is capable of doing. Goals should not be so difficult that the athlete will fail to take them seriously or will experience failure and frustration in meeting them. It is therefore important for you to set goals in relation to each athlete's ability. The goals should be set so that they are difficult enough to challenge athletes but realistic enough to be achievable.

> **Key Principle**
> Goals should be specific, challenging, and set up in staircase fashion, with short-term goals leading toward long-term objectives.

3. *Set short-term as well as long-range goals.* Breaking down any long-term goal into smaller more attainable goals is conducive to achievement and success. Short-term goals are important because they allow athletes to see immediate improvements in performance and thereby enhance motivation. Without short-term goals, athletes can lose sight of their long-range goals, and the subgoals needed to attain them.

One way to understand the relationship between short- and long-range goals is in terms of a staircase. The top stair represents the athlete's long-range goal or objective, and the lowest stair is the present level of performance. The steps in between represent a progression of short-term goals of increasing difficulty that lead from the bottom to the top of the stairs. The short-term goals allow athletes to enjoy successes and accomplishments as they move toward the top of the stairs. This idea is captured by the old saying "Yard by yard it is awfully hard, but inch by inch it becomes a cinch!"

4. *Set performance goals as opposed to outcome goals.* As we noted in Chapter 2, our society places tremendous emphasis on the outcome of athletic events, and it is not surprising that many athletes are used to setting only outcome goals such as winning or beating a particular opponent. The problem with outcome goals, however, is that athletes have only partial control over them. An athlete may achieve the best performance ever and yet fail to achieve the outcome goal of winning an event because someone performed even better. It is far better to set goals in terms of personal performance standards, for then success is seen in terms of athletes exceeding their own goals rather than surpassing the performance of others. When winning (outcome) becomes secondary to achieving their own personal goals, athletes are much more motivated to practice. Practices give athletes the opportunity to work toward their personal goals with assistance from the coach. Athletes do not judge themselves as having succeeded or failed purely on the basis of whether they have won or lost, but in terms of their achievement of the specific performance and behavioral goals they have set. Thus the amount of personal satisfaction that athletes achieve from sport does not need to be tied to winning. Athletes at all levels of ability can enjoy success through attainment of their personal goals. Stating goals in such terms also helps athletes to learn the valuable lesson that winning has more to do with *doing their best* than *being the best*. In the words of football coach Tom Osborne, "Our goal is not stated in terms of winning, since that is not something we control, but rather, to execute as best we can."

5. *Express goals in positive rather than negative terms.* In line with the *positive approach* to coaching discussed in Chapter 4, it is best to set goals positively (number or percentage of plays carried out correctly) rather than negatively (number or percentage of mistakes reduced). This positive goal-setting procedure helps athletes focus on success instead of failure.

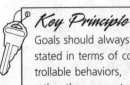

Key Principle

Goals should always be stated in terms of controllable behaviors, rather than uncontrollable outcomes, and they should always be positive in nature.

6. *Set goals for both practices and competition.* It is just as important, if not more so, to set goals for practice sessions as it is for competitive events. Practices are the times when

athletes develop and hone their skills. According to professional basketball coach Pat Riley, "The will to prepare is the key to winning. You've got to pay the price. You play like you practice."

When practice becomes meaningful as a result of being tied in with specific goals, athletes become more involved in what is going on, and practice time can be used much more productively. Moreover, setting specific goals related to practice and tracking progress toward them help reduce the drudgery of practice and makes it more meaningful for the athlete. During practice, each athlete can work toward specific performance goals that are geared to his or her areas of strength and weakness. Thus one football player's goals may be keyed to improving his blocking, while another's may relate to tackling.

Since the presumed goal of every competitor is to win, it might seem meaningless to set additional goals during competition itself. However, such goals can be very useful in that they provide one means by which winning will be achieved. For example, a basketball team can set a team goal for a game, such as holding the opponent's best player to 15 points, outrebounding the other team, or limiting turnovers to no more than 10. By focusing on the attainment of specific performance goals, coaches can create a "game within the game" in which athletes can be successful in some important respects, even if they are not victorious in terms of the final score. Many coaches have found that this technique helps prevent players from being discouraged if the team does not win and helps promote steady improvement in the team's play.

7. *Identify specific goal achievement strategies.* All too often, goals are not accomplished because athletes fail to identify and commit themselves to goal achievement strategies. Setting goals without identifying ways of achieving them is not very effective. Thus a basketball player who wants to improve his free throw percentage by 5% may choose an achievement strategy of shooting 30 additional free throws after practice each day.

8. *Record goals, achievement strategies, and target dates for attaining goals.* Once (a) specific goals have been set, (b) achievement strategies have been decided upon by the athlete and coach, and (c) target dates for goal accomplishment have been established, these should be writ-

ten down so that they can be referred to frequently. Some coaches actually establish a formal contract with players to keep them focused on the activity and committed to it.

9. *Set up a performance feedback or goal evaluation system.* Goal-setting research indicates that performance feedback is absolutely necessary if goals are to enhance performance. Therefore athletes must receive feedback about how their present performance is related to both short- and long-range goals. Without such feedback, athletes cannot track their progress toward goals and may be unable to see improvement that is actually occurring. Former University of Washington football coach Don James was a strong believer in performance feedback: "The best way to build confidence in your players is to show improvement through statistics."

> **Key Principle**
>
> Goal setting only works when it includes well-defined strategies for goal attainment, specific performance feedback, and a method for measuring and recording progress.

Feedback can also correct misconceptions. Athletes, like other people, often have distorted perceptions of their own behavior. Objective evidence in the form of statistics or numbers can help correct such misconceptions and may help motivate corrective action. For example, it can be a sobering experience for a basketball player who fancies herself a great ball handler to find out that she has more turnovers than assists.

Feedback also creates internal consequences by causing athletes to experience positive (or negative) feelings about themselves. An athlete who is dissatisfied with his or her level of performance will experience feelings of self-satisfaction that function as positive reinforcement when subsequent feedback indicates improvement. The feelings of pride and self-confidence that arise can be even more important than external reinforcement from the coach in bringing out improved performance. Promoting self-motivation in athletes also reduces the need for coaches to reinforce or punish. When feedback is public, as in the posting of statistics, the actual or anticipated reactions of others can serve as an additional motivator of increased effort and performance.

10. *Goal-setting programs are most effective when they are supported by those individuals who are important in the athlete's life.* This typically

includes the coach, teammates, and the athlete's family. Therefore it is important that you promote the recognition, encouragement, and support of individual and team movement toward goals. You yourself are a central figure in providing such support.

Some Pitfalls to Avoid

In addition to the goal-setting principles presented above, there are some things to avoid. It is not particularly difficult to set up a goal-setting program. However, the preceding guidelines suggested some ways in which problems can arise when goal-setting procedures are used. One such problem occurs when too many goals are set too soon. If too many goals are set, athletes cannot properly monitor performance, or they find it very difficult to do so. A much better procedure is to rank the goals and focus attention on the one or two goals that are most important.

A second problem arises in setting goals that are too general. We have emphasized the importance of setting specific, measurable goals. The general principle here is that if you can't measure the goal in terms of specific numbers, it is too vague and general to be used effectively. It is important to remember that performance goals are preferable to outcome goals because the athlete has greater control over them.

> *Key Principle*
> Coaches should avoid setting too many goals, goals that are not specific enough, and goals that are forced on athletes.

Finally, you may encounter athletes who have very negative attitudes toward goal setting and do not want to participate in such a program. It is best not to force such athletes to participate. More often than not, they will observe the benefits and enjoyment that other athletes are experiencing as a result of goal setting and will come on board later on.

Putting Goal Setting to Work

To be successful in carrying out a goal-setting program, coaches must employ some sort of goal-setting system or procedure. The simplest and most effective system has three main phases: (a) the planning phase, (b) the meeting phase, and (c) the follow-up or evaluation phase.

The Planning Phase

Setting up a goal-setting program obviously requires a good deal of planning on your part. First of all, you must identify individual and team needs. These may be in a variety of areas including performance, conditioning, sportsmanship, care of equipment, relations among teammates, and so forth. Once the most important of these are decided upon, coaches must decide how they can help their athletes achieve these goals. In other words, you yourself must engage in a goal-setting program in terms of identifying goals and specifying how you are going to help athletes attain them.

Meeting With Athletes

After goals have been decided upon, it is important that the coach communicate these to the athletes and indicate why they are important. How detailed you get in this meeting will of course depend upon the level of maturity of your athletes. With older and more experienced athletes, you may choose to meet with each one individually after the general meeting in order to decide upon goals and strategies. For younger athletes, team rather than individual goals may be more appropriate, but it is essential that these goals be very specific and measurable.

> **Key Principle**
> Goal setting requires commitment on the part of the coach as well as the athletes, but its rewards are well worth the effort.

It may be necessary to involve athletes in the measurement of behaviors relating to specific goals. For example, an athlete who is not currently playing in a soccer match may keep track of the number of passes made before each shot if one of the goals is to work the ball around the defense before shooting.

Follow-Up/Evaluation

To ensure that movement toward goals and possible revision of goals can occur, it is a good idea to set up several evaluation meetings with individuals, subgroups of athletes, or the entire team. A critical part of the entire process is the feedback procedure you choose to employ. The procedure should allow you and your athletes to see clearly where things stand in relation to the goals that have been set. If your athletes are mature enough, you might require that they monitor their own target behaviors to supplement whatever statistics you might use to chart progress toward goals.

When coaches help athletes to set realistic goals and provide ways for them to attain those goals, youngsters inevitably experience more success and feel more competent. By becoming more competent, they gain in self-confidence and become less fearful of failure. Perhaps most important, they discover that commitment to goals helps lead to success. They also learn with your help that failure indicates they should try harder, not that they are unworthy. Deemphasizing winning and emphasizing attainment of personal and team goals can greatly increase the positive impact that a coach can have on the athlete's performance and enjoyment of the sport.

Counteracting Stress and Teaching Mental Toughness

Sports challenge us. They place demands on us. The athletic setting is one in which we can test the limits of our abilities in competition both with ourselves and others. Many times we are required to put ourselves on the line and to test our mental as well as physical limits.

These features of the sport environment not only attract people to sports, but they also serve as potential sources of stress. The physical and mental tests that are opportunities and challenges to some can be psychological threats to others. As we noted earlier, some athletes have a positive drive to succeed, and they regard pressure situations as challenges and rise to the occasion. Others, unfortunately, are motivated primarily by a fear of failing. When faced with the pressures of athletic competition, they are likely to be paralyzed by their fear and to "choke."

We are convinced that these different motivational styles can be strongly influenced by an athlete's early experiences in sports. As a coach you are in a position to influence the outlooks and attitudes that your athletes develop toward the challenges of competition. Since these challenges are similar in many respects to other challenges the young athlete will experience in life, the attitudes that you help to establish can have an influence that extends far beyond the sport setting.

The differences that exist in the ability of people to cope successfully with stressful situations are learned primarily during the childhood and adolescent years. Athletics can be an important arena in which

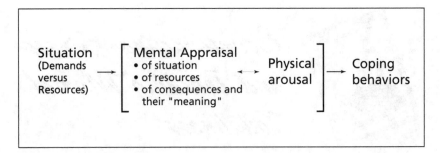

Figure 6.1 *The nature of stress.*

such skills are learned. In a sense, the athletic experience can be a sort of laboratory for trying out and mastering ways of dealing with stress.

Understanding Athletic Stress

We typically use the term *stress* in two different but related ways. First, we use the term to refer to *situations* in our lives that place physical or psychological demands on us. Second, we use the term to refer to our mental, emotional, and behavioral *responses* to these demanding situations. These responses include such emotions as tension, anxiety, anger, and depression.

In Figure 6.1, we present an analysis of stress that takes both the situation and the athlete's reactions into account. As you can see, four major elements are involved.

The first element is the external situation that is making some sort of physical or psychological demand on the person. Typically we view our emotions as being directly triggered by these "pressure" situations. This, however, is not the case. The true emotional triggers are not in the external situation but in our minds, in what we have called *mental appraisal*. This evaluation process has several parts. First of all, we appraise the nature of the situation and the demands it is placing upon us. At the same time, we appraise the resources that we have to deal with it. We judge, in other words, how capable we are of coping with the situation. We also judge the probable consequences of coping or failing to cope with the situation and the meaning of those consequences for us.

The emotional responses that we call stress are likely to occur when we view ourselves as incapable of coping with a high-demand situation that has potentially harmful consequences for us. In response to such appraisals our body becomes physically aroused, with pounding heart, rapid breathing, elevated blood pressure, tight and trembling muscles, and so on. This is part of the body's natural defense system, and it mobilizes us to respond to the emergency.

The fourth element in our analysis of stress involves the behaviors that the person uses in order to try to cope with demands of the situation. Responses may be mental, as when a quarterback tries to figure out which play to call, or they may be physical or social responses, such as shooting a free throw or dealing with an angry opponent.

How Stress Affects Young Athletes

Fear and anxiety are the emotions that are most frequently experienced as part of the athletic stress response. These are unpleasant states that most people try to avoid. There is evidence that this is precisely what many stress-ridden young athletes do. Avoiding or dropping out of sports is one of the ways some children escape from an activity they find threatening rather than pleasant.

In addition to influencing decisions about entering and/or continuing to participate, competitive stress can detract from athletes' enjoyment of sports. Instead of a challenging, fulfilling activity, sports can become a threat to self-esteem and can rob children of the pleasures they should derive from participation. Eventually this can take its toll on the athlete and produce burnout. Burnout is a legitimate concern, because burned out athletes often show depression and loss of drive and energy that carries over into other areas of their lives.

Key Principle

Athletic stress can not only detract from the fun of sports but also impair performance and negatively affect the physical well-being of young athletes.

Stress affects not only how athletes feel, but also how they perform. All of us have seen athletes fall apart or "choke" under high levels of stress. When arousal is absent or extremely low, athletes frequently describe themselves as "flat" and do not perform as well as they are able. Some degree of arousal is usually needed for good performance. But at extremely high levels, arousal begins to interfere with performance. Research has shown that the more complicated or difficult the task, the less arousal it takes to interfere with performance. High-stress athletes who cannot control their emotions are likely to experience higher-than-optimal levels of arousal and to perform poorly. The failure experiences that result only serve to reinforce these athletes' fears and undermine their confidence even more. Thus a vicious circle involving anxiety, impaired performance, and increased anxiety can result. In pressure situations, high-stress athletes have difficulty concentrating and thinking clearly. This also serves to interfere with performance. Many young athletes fail to achieve their potential in sports because of their inability to control their anxiety.

Stress can affect physical well-being as well as performance. The physical nature of the stress response taxes the resources of the body and appears to increase susceptibility to illness and disease. Disruption of youngsters' eating and sleep patterns can occur. This is surely a high and unnecessary price to pay for the pursuit of athletic excellence!

Finally, research has shown that stress is related to an increased likelihood of athletic injury. Sports medicine specialists have also observed that athletes who find participation stressful and unpleasant often appear to take longer to recover from injuries. It may be that in some cases, an athlete finds in an injury a temporary and legitimate haven from the stress of competition.

We see, then, that stress can have many effects on athletes of all ages and that most of these effects are negative (Figure 6.2). Thus athletes who develop coping skills that allow them to bear up under the pressure of competition, to be mentally tough in the face of athletic challenge and adversity, have a definite advantage.

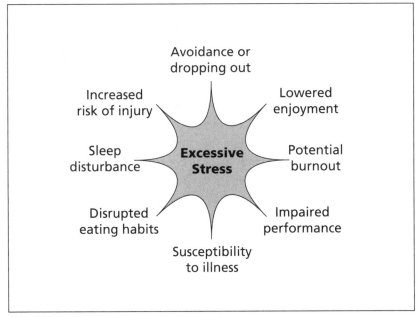

Figure 6.2 *Negative effects of excessive stress in youth sports.*

Mental Toughness As Teachable Skills

One of the highest compliments that can be paid to an athlete is to be labeled "mentally tough." Coaches speak of mental toughness as if it were a quality that a person either has or does not have. In reality, however, mental toughness is not something we are born with; rather, it is a set of specific, learned attitudes and skills.

The specific skills that consitute what we call mental toughness fall within the brackets of the stress model described above. Mentally tough athletes mentally appraise themselves and pressure situations in ways that arouse a positive desire to achieve rather than a fear of failure. Freedom from

Key Principle

Mental toughness is best viewed as a set of specific, learnable skills that can give a young-ster the winning edge not only in sports, but in other life settings as well.

the disruptive effects of fear of failure allows them to concentrate on the task instead of worrying about the terrible things that will happen if they fail in the situation. Another specific skill that contributes to mental toughness is the ability to keep physical arousal within manageable limits. Somehow these athletes are able to "psych up" with enough arousal to optimize their performance without being "psyched out" by excessive arousal. What mental toughness amounts to, therefore, is specific ways of viewing the competitive situation and skills relating to self-control of emotion and concentration.

The core of mental toughness is the ability to control emotional responses and concentrate on what has to be done in pressure situations. The mentally tough athlete is in control of emotions and is calm and relaxed under fire. Such athletes do not avoid pressure; they are challenged by it. They are at their best when the pressure is on and the odds are against them. Being put to the test is not a threat, but another opportunity to achieve. Mentally tough athletes are able to concentrate on the task at hand in situations where less capable athletes lose their focus of attention. They rarely fall victim to their own or others' self-defeating thoughts and ideas, and they are not easily intimidated. Finally, they are mentally resilient and have the ability to bounce back from adversity, their determination to succeed coming across as a quiet self-assurance.

It is no accident that mentally tough athletes tend to get the most out of their physical ability. Their level of performance seems to be more consistent, and they have a tendency to perform at their best when pressure is the greatest.

As a coach, you are in a position to help your young athletes develop the skills that comprise mental toughness. In doing so, you can help sport to serve as a catalyst in their personal development.

Reducing Stress and Building Mental Toughness
Fear of Failure: The Athlete's Worst Enemy

Aside from fears of physical injury that produce stress for some athletes, most athletic stress arises from the fact that sport is an important social situation. The athlete's performance is visible to everyone pre-

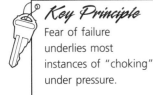

Key Principle
Fear of failure underlies most instances of "choking" under pressure.

sent, and it is constantly being evaluated by the athlete and by significant people in his or her life. Many athletes dread the possibility of failure and fear the disapproval of others. Some feel that their athletic performance is a reflection of their basic self-worth, and they therefore have a great need to avoid failing. They are convinced that failure will diminish them in their own eyes and in the eyes of others.

Fear of failure is the athlete's worst enemy. The thinking of high-stress athletes is dominated by negative thoughts and worries about failing. Unchecked, these concerns with failure undermine confidence, enthusiasm, the willingness to invest and persist, and, most important, the athlete's belief in self. It is these thoughts that transform the competitive athletic situation from what should be a welcome challenge to a threatening and unpleasant pressure-cooker. It is these thoughts that trigger the high physical arousal that interferes with performance and interfere with the ability to concentrate fully on the task at hand.

The ideas that underlie fear of failure do not arise in a vacuum. They almost always have been communicated to youngsters by their parents or by other important adults, including coaches. This is not surprising, because the basic beliefs underlying such ideas are widely accepted in our culture, which emphasizes achievement as a measure of personal worth. In our society an untold number of children fall victim to their parents' demands that they perform exactly as expected, and to condemnations when they fail. Too often the child's achievements are viewed as an indication of the worth of the parents, and failure brings reprisals based on the parent's feelings that they are to blame or that they themselves are inadequate. For many children love becomes a premium handed out on the basis of what a child can *do* rather than simply who he or she *is*.

Key Principle
Fear of failure is easy to create, but hard to get rid of because it is reinforced by widely-accepted cultural beliefs.

The fastest and easiest way to create fear of failure in a child is to punish unsuccessful performance by criticizing it or by withholding love from the youngster. Under such circumstances, children learn to dread failure because it is associated with punishment or rejection. They also learn to fear and avoid situations in which they might fail. The unfortunate lesson they learn is that their worth and lovability depend on how well they perform. Instead of trying to achieve in order to reap the built-in rewards of achievement and mastery, children strive to perform well to avoid failure. They begin to measure themselves by their performance; and if their performance is inadequate they usually consider their total being inadequate. A child can ultimately become so fearful of failing that all attempts to succeed are abandoned. This almost guarantees that the child cannot meet the standards she or he has set and it serves only to reinforce feelings of inadequacy. In the words of coach John Wooden, "Because they fear failure, many people never try and thereby rob themselves of opportunities to be successful."

Even though you enter into the life of a child athlete for a limited period of time, you can as a coach have a dramatic impact in helping the young athlete develop a positive desire to achieve rather than a fear of failure. Earlier we described four elements in the stress cycle: (a) the situation, (b) mental appraisal of the situation, (c) physical arousal, and (d) coping behaviors. Coaches can influence all four of these elements in ways that reduce stress and build mental toughness.

Reducing Situational Stress

The first way you can reduce stress is to change aspects of the situation that place unnecessary demands on young athletes. We are all well aware that coaches and parents can create stress by their actions. Many young athletes experience unnecessary stress because adults put undue pressure on them to perform well. Coaches who are punishing and abusive to children can create a very stressful and unenjoyable environment. Similarly, parents who yell at their children during games or withdraw their love if the young athlete lets them down can create a situation in which the youngster "runs scared" much of the time. Eliminating such actions by coaches and parents can reduce unnecessary stress.

The behavioral guidelines presented in Chapter 4 can help you reduce stress and create a more enjoyable atmosphere. The *positive approach* emphasized in the guidelines is specifically designed to counteract the conditions that create fear of failure. The same is true of the philosophy of winning discussed in Chapter 2. By promoting this philosophy of winning through use of the behavioral guidelines, you stand an excellent chance of creating a sport environment in which children can enjoy themselves, develop their skills in an atmosphere of encouragement and reinforcement, and experience positive and supportive relationships with their coach and teammates.

One of the most important differences between the *positive approach* to coaching and the *negative approach* is the kind of motivation that they produce. In the negative approach, punishment and criticism are used liberally in an attempt to "stamp out" mistakes. This approach operates by creating fear of failing. In contrast, the positive approach favored in CET makes use of encouragement and reinforcement in an attempt to strengthen desirable behaviors. The motivation this kind of an approach develops is a positive desire to achieve and succeed rather than a negative fear of making mistakes. Thus, while both approaches may result in improvements in performance, they do so for different reasons and create different types of *motivation*. Under the positive approach, athletes come to see successful performance as an opportunity to experience a reward. On the other hand, the athlete who has been coached by the negative approach comes to view successful performance as a way of avoiding punishment. It is not surprising that athletes coached with a positive approach come to see pressure situations as challenges and opportunities, whereas those subjected to a negative approach see the same kinds of situations as threats.

Key Principle

Coaches can be either a source of stress by using the negative approach, or a buffer against its harmful effects by adopting the of Coach Effectiveness Training.

Parents can at times be a significant source of stress for young athletes. As a coach you may be in a position to help parents correct stress-producing behavior patterns. Ideally you would like your athletes' parents to be reinforcing the attitudes and outlooks about competition that you are communicating through your words and actions. In Chapter 9 we discuss some ways in which you can accomplish this goal.

Increasing the Athlete's Resources: Skills and Social Support

Stress is experienced when we perceive an imbalance between the demands of the situation and the resources that we have to cope with the demands. It follows that another approach to reducing stress is to increase the young athlete's resources. Two types of resources are very important: (a) the skills that the athlete possesses, and (b) the amount of support that the athlete receives from important people such as the coach, teammates, and parents. In your role as coach, you are in a position to influence both classes of resources.

It is quite natural to feel insecure when we don't have the skills needed to cope with a situation. Many young athletes experience this insecurity when they first begin to learn a sport. As their athletic skills increase, they become better able to deal with the demands of the athletic situation, and their stress decreases. Thus, being an effective teacher and working with young athletes to improve their skills is one way that you can help reduce athletic stress. Here again, we strongly recommend the positive approach, since we feel this is the most effective way to teach skills and create a positive learning environment. As athletes become more confident in their abilities, they see themselves as prepared to cope with the demands of the athletic situation.

> **Key Principle**
> Athletic stress can be combatted by mastery of sport skills and by an environment that provides plenty of social support.

There is abundant scienific evidence that the positive approach can create better relationships among coaches and athletes. Our research as well as studies of team building have shown that coaches who use this approach have more cohesive teams on which players like one another more. By using your own "reinforcement power" to encourage teammates to support one another, you help create a higher level of social support for all of your players. When a team can pull together and support one another in pressure situations, this kind of social support can help reduce the level of stress experienced by individual athletes.

Developing Winning Attitudes Toward Competition

As noted earlier, the term *stress* is used in two different ways. One use of the term relates to *situations* that place high demands on us. The

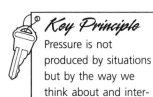

Key Principle

Pressure is not produced by situations but by the way we think about and interpret those situations.

other refers to our *response* to such situations. The importance of this distinction becomes particularly clear when we deal with the role of mental processes in stress. There is a big difference between *pressure situations* and *feeling pressure*. Mentally tough athletes perform well in pressure situations precisely because they have eliminated the pressure. They report that although intel-

lectually they are aware that they are in a very tough situation they really don't feel the pressure on the inside. There is no way to eliminate pressure *situations*; they will always be there because they are a natural part of competition. This does not mean, however, that athletes have to respond to such situations by experiencing high levels of stress and getting "psyched out."

Mentally tough competitors manage pressure well largely because they have become disciplined thinkers. Either consciously or unconsciously they have made the connection in their own heads between what they think and how much pressure they feel during competition. They have learned (often the hard way) that thoughts like these produce pressure:

- "What if I don't do well?"

- "I can't blow it now."

- "I can't stand this pressure."

- "I'll never live it down if I lose."

- "If I miss these free throws, what will everyone say?"

- "If I don't sink this putt, I'll lose everything!"

On the other hand, mentally tough athletes think like this in pressure situations:

- "I'm going to do the best I can and let the cards fall where they may."

- "All I can do is give 100%. No one can do more."

- "This is supposed to be fun, and I'm going to make sure it is."

- "I don't have to put pressure on myself. All I have to do is focus on doing my job the best I know how."

- "I'm going to focus on the good things that will happen when I make the play."

- "I'm concentrating on performing, rather than winning or losing."

The first set of statements causes an athlete to react to adversity with bitterness, frustration, and anxiety. The second set of statements focuses attention where it should be: on giving maximum effort and concentrating totally on what has to be done. Pressure situations become welcome opportunities, rather than dire threats for mentally tough athletes. The bottom line is that the fundamental difference between mentally tough athletes and "chokers" is the way they choose to construct the situation in their heads. Situations are not nervous, tense, or anxious—people are! The sooner you can help athletes to realize that pressure comes from within and not from outside, the sooner they can start shutting it down.

> *Key Principle*
>
> "When an athlete can start loving adversity, I know I've got a competitor!"
>
> Al McGuire, former Marquette University basketball coach

One of the great benefits of sports as a training ground for mental toughness is that the consequences of failure are temporary and unlikely to have a long-term impact on the future of a child (as failing in school might). This places you in a great position to help your young athletes develop a healthy philosophy about achievement and an ability to tolerate failure and setbacks when they occur. The starting point for such training is the philosophy, described in Chapter 2, that great coaches like John Wooden and Vince Lombardi instilled in their athletes. These coaches developed mentally tough athletes and teams by realizing that an obsession with winning is self-defeating because it places the cart before the horse. They realized that effort should be directed not toward winning but toward performing to the very best of the athlete's ability at the time. Doing the very best one can at any moment should always be the focus and the goal. Winning will take care of itself; the only thing that can be directly controlled is *effort*. Mental toughness arises in the realization that "I am performing against myself, not someone else. I will always be my own toughest opponent, and winning the battle with myself paves the way for winning the contest with my opponent."

Here are some specific attitudes that can be communicated to players by a coach.

1. *Sports should be fun.* Emphasize to your young athletes that sports and other activities in life are enjoyable for the playing whether you win or lose. Athletes should be participating, first and foremost, to have fun.

2. *Anything worth achieving is rarely easy.* There is nothing disgraceful about it being a long and difficult process to master something. Becoming the best athlete one can be is not an achievement to be had merely for the asking. Practice, practice, and still more practice is needed to master any sport. Coach Joe Paterno always maintained that "The will to win is important, but the will to *prepare* to win is essential."

3. *Mistakes are a necessary part of learning anything well.* Very simply, if we don't make mistakes we probably won't learn. Stress to your athletes that mistakes, rather than being things to avoid at all costs, are stepping stones to success. They give us the information we need to adjust and improve. The only true failure is a failure to learn from our mistakes.

4. *Effort is what counts.* Emphasize and praise effort as well as outcome. Communicate repeatedly to your athletes that all you ask of them is that they give total effort. Through your actions and your words, show your athletes that they are just as important to you when trying and failing as when succeeding. If maximum effort is acceptable to you it can also become acceptable to them. Above all, do not punish or withdraw love and approval when they don't perform up to expectations. It is such punishment that builds fear of failure.

5. *Do not confuse worth with performance.* Help your athletes to distinguish what they do from what they are. A valuable lesson for children to learn is that they should never identify their worth as people with any particular part of themselves, such as their competence in

Key Principle

Coaches should not allow youngsters to define their personal worth in terms of their performance on the athletic field or court.

sports, their school performance, or their physical appearance. You can further this process by demonstrating your own ability to accept your athletes unconditionally as people of value, even when you are communicating that you don't approve of some behavior. Also, show your athletes that you can gracefully accept your own mistakes and failures. Show and tell them that as a fallible human being you can accept the fact that despite your best efforts you are going to occasionally bungle things. If your athletes can learn from you to accept and like themselves, they will not unduly require the approval of others in order to feel worthwhile.

6. *Pressure is something you put on yourself.* Help your athletes to see competitive situations as exciting self-challenges rather than as threats. Emphasize that they can choose how they want to think about pressure situations. The above attitudes will help them to develop an outlook on pressure that transforms it into a challenge and an opportunity to test themselves and to achieve something worthwhile.

7. *Try to like and respect your opponents.* Some coaches and athletes think that proper motivation comes from anger or hatred for the opponent. We disagree. Sports should promote sportsmanship and an appreciation that opponents, far from being the "enemy," are fellow athletes who make it possible to compete. Hatred can only breed stress and fear. In terms of emotional arousal, fear and anger are indistinguishable patterns of physiologic responses. Thus the arousal of anger can become the arousal of fear if things begin to go badly during a contest. Former Nebraska football coach Tom Osborne preached respect for the opponent because, in his experience "Athletes who play in a generally relaxed environment where there's goodwill toward their opponents are less fearful and play better."

When children learn to enjoy sports for their own sake, when their goal becomes to *do their best* rather than *be the best*, and when they avoid the trap of defining their self-worth in terms of their performance or the approval of others, then their way of viewing themselves and their world is one that helps prevent stress. Such children are success-oriented rather than failure-avoidant. They strive to succeed rather than to try to avoid failure. Coaches who impart these lessons to their young athletes give them a priceless gift that will benefit them in many of their endeavors in life.

Controlling Arousal: Teaching Your Athletes Relaxation Skills

Coaches increasingly recognize the importance of psychological as well as physical skills. Despite this recognition, however, coaches have been given little information on how to teach psychological skills. It is no accident, therefore, that coaches spend almost all of their time teaching their players techniques and strategies, while pretty much leaving the learning of psychological skills to chance.

One very useful psychological skill that athletes can be taught by their coaches is relaxation. Most athletes perform better when they are in a moderately relaxed state. As noted earlier, a moderate level of emotional arousal can psych athletes up to perform more efficiently. On the other hand, high levels of arousal can interfere with thought and behavior patterns. Few athletes can perform well when they are all tensed up as a result of high arousal.

The ability to remain calm in a stressful situation, or at least to prevent arousal from climbing out of control, is a useful stress management skill. Many athletes have found that they can learn to prevent or control high levels of tension through training in muscle relaxation skills. Because one cannot be relaxed and tense at the same time, voluntary relaxation gives athletes the ability to turn off or tone down tension. Although it is clearly a skill and must be learned through work and practice, most people can be trained to relax.

Relaxation training actually has two benefits. The first is the ability to reduce or control the level of arousal, but the second is equally important. In the course of relaxation training, people become more sensitive to what is going on inside their bodies and are better able to detect arousal in its beginning stages. When they can detect the early warning signs of developing tension, they can plug in their coping responses at an early stage before the tension gets out of control.

We have been training athletes in relaxation skills for many years. We have found that children as young as 5 or 6 years of age can be

Key Principle
Mastering coping skills at an early age can benefit a child throughout life, and coaches can teach one of these skills through relaxation training.

trained in relaxation, and they can then use these skills to reduce tension and anxiety. Our experience has been that children who learn this and other stress-coping skills (such as the attitudes described earlier) show a marked increase in self-confidence and are less reluctant to tackle difficult situations. They apply these skills not only in athletics, but also in other important life situations.

We now describe a training program that you can use to train your athletes (and yourself, if you wish) in relaxation skills. The approach that we describe involves training through a process of voluntarily tensing and relaxing various muscle groups. The goal is to learn voluntary relaxation skills while gaining increased sensitivity to body tension. We find that within about a week of conscientious training, most people can increase their ability to relax themselves and reduce tension.

If you wish to help your athletes learn relaxation, we recommend that you go through the exercises on your own several times to become familiar with the procedure. Then you can easily guide your youngsters through the exercises until they become familiar enough with them to practice without your help. We have taught these procedures to many coaches who continue to use them regularly as part of their practice sessions.

We recommend that the relaxation exercises be practiced at least once and preferably twice a day until they are mastered. They can be carried out in chairs or on a fairly soft floor (that is, on a carpeted floor or gym mats).

Explain to your athletes why they are learning this procedure, and point out to them that many champion athletes have learned this skill.

Key Principle
Mentally tough athletes have the ability to relax themselves quickly, even in the heat of competition.

As you guide the athletes through the exercises, use a slow, relaxed tone of voice. Give the athletes plenty of time to experience the sensations, and make sure that they are doing the breathing part of the exercises correctly. The goal of the training is to combine relaxation, exhalation, and the mental command to relax repeatedly so that the athlete will be able to induce relaxation by exhaling and mentally telling himself or herself to relax.

In our training procedure, we start by concentrating on the hands and arms; move to the legs, stomach and chest, back muscles, and neck and jaw; and finish up with the facial and scalp muscles. Here are the steps.

1. While sitting comfortably, bend your arms at the elbow. Now make a hard fist with both hands, and bend your wrists downward while simultaneously tensing the muscles of your upper arms. This will produce a state of tension in your hands, forearms, and upper arms. Hold this tension for 5 seconds and study it carefully, then slowly let the tension out halfway while concentrating on the sensations in your arms and fingers as tension decreases. Hold the tension at the halfway point for 5 seconds, and then slowly let the tension out the rest of the way and rest your arms comfortably in your lap. Concentrate carefully on the contrast between the tension which you have just experienced and the relaxation which deepens as you voluntarily relax the muscles for an additional 10 to 15 seconds. As you breathe normally, concentrate on those muscles and give yourself the mental command to relax each time you exhale. Do this for seven to ten breaths.

If you train your athletes, here is a sample of how you can phrase the instructions when presenting this exercise.

> Do you know what uncooked spaghetti feels like? (They'll tell you hard, dry, and brittle. You can even have a piece with you to demonstrate.) That's almost what our muscles are like when we're all tensed up. You can't play sports when your muscles are like that. Now, what does cooked spaghetti feel like? Yes, it's soft and supple, like our muscles are when they're relaxed. What we're going to do is to learn to make our muscles like cooked spaghetti so we can quickly get rid of tension and play relaxed.

> We're going to start out with the arms and hands. What I'd like you to do while keeping your eyes closed is to bend your arms and make a fist like this. [*Demonstrate*]

> Now make a hard fist and tense those muscles in your arms hard. Notice the tension and the pulling throughout your arm as those muscles stretch and bunch up like rubber bands. Focus on those

feelings of tension in your arms and hands. They're like uncooked spaghetti—hard and stiff.

[*After 5 seconds*] Now slowly begin to let that tension out halfway, and concentrate very carefully on the feeling in your arms and hands as you do that. Now hold the tension at the halfway point and notice how your arms and hands are less tense than before but that there is still tension present.

[*After 5 seconds*] Now slowly let the tension out all the way and just let your arms and hands become completely relaxed, just letting go and becoming more and more relaxed, feeling all the tension draining away as the muscles let go and become completely relaxed. And now, each time you breathe out, let your mind tell your body to relax, and concentrate on relaxing the muscles even more. That's good . . . just let go. Let those muscles become soft and supple, like cooked spaghetti.

2. Tense the calf and thigh muscles in your legs. You can do this by straightening out your legs hard while pointing your toes downward. Hold the tension for 5 seconds, then slowly let it out halfway. Hold the halfway point for an additional 5 seconds, and then slowly let the tension out all the way and concentrate on relaxing the muscles as completely as possible. Again, pay careful attention to the feelings of tension and relaxation as they develop. Finish by giving the muscles the mental command "Relax" each time you exhale (seven to ten times), and concentrate on relaxing them as deeply as possible.

3. Cross the palms of your hands in front of your chest and press them together to tense the chest and shoulder muscles. At the same time, tense your stomach muscles hard. As before, hold the tension for 5 seconds, then slowly let the tension out halfway and focus on the decreasing levels of tension as you do so. Hold again for 5 seconds at the halfway point and then slowly let the tension out completely. Again, do the breathing procedure with the mental command to deepen the relaxation in your stomach, chest, and shoulder muscles.

4. Arch your back and push your shoulders back as far as possible to tense your upper and lower back muscles. (Be careful not to tense these muscles too hard.) Repeat the standard procedure of slowly releasing the tension halfway, then all the way. Finish by doing the breathing

exercise and mental command as you relax your back muscles as deeply as possible.

5. Tense your neck and jaw muscles by thrusting your jaw outward and drawing the corners of your mouth back. Release the tension slowly to the halfway point, hold for 5 seconds there, and then slowly release the tension in these muscles all the way. Let your head droop into a comfortable position and your jaw slacken as you concentrate on totally relaxing these muscles with your breathing exercise and mental command. (You can also tense your neck muscles in other ways, such as bending your neck forward, backward, or to one side. Experiment to find out the way that's best for you. Tense your jaw at the same time.)

6. Wrinkle your forehead and scalp to tense these muscles. Hold the tension for 5 seconds, then release it halfway for an additional 5 seconds. Then relax your eyes completely. Focus on relaxing your facial and scalp muscles completely, and use your breathing exercise and mental command.

7. While sitting in a totally relaxed position, take a series of short inhalations, about one per second, until your chest is filled and tense. Hold each for about 5 seconds, then exhale slowly while thinking silently to yourself "Relax." Most people can produce a deeply relaxed state by doing this. Repeat this exercise three times.

8. Finish off your relaxation practice by concentrating on breathing comfortably into your abdomen (rather than into your chest area). Simply let your stomach fill with air as you inhale, and deepen your relaxation as you exhale. Abdominal breathing is far more relaxing than breathing into the chest.

As you guide your athletes through the exercises, you can practice them yourself. You will find relaxation very useful in your own life. It not only serves as a weapon against tension and stress, but it produces an enjoyable state in its own right.

Mental Imagery and Performance Enhancement

The night before a game, I lie down, close my eyes, relax my body, and prepare myself for the game. I go through the entire lineup of the other team, one batter at a time. I visualize exactly how I am going to pitch to each hitter, and I see and feel myself throwing exactly the pitches that I want to throw. Before I ever begin to warm up at the ball park, I've faced all of the opposition's hitters four times and I've gotten my body ready for exactly what it is I want to do.

The speaker was Nolan Ryan, one of the great pitchers of all time. Ryan maintained that the mental skills he had developed over the years were every bit as important to his success as his physical talent. Among those skills, two were of primary importance. One was the ability to relax and maintain his concentration under even the most adverse conditions. The second was the ability to program himself through mental rehearsal.

It goes by a variety of names: *visualization, mental rehearsal,* or *imagery.* We prefer the terms *mental rehearsal* or *imagery* to *visualization* because mental rehearsal involves far more than simply "seeing with the mind's eye." Effective mental rehearsal involves all of the senses, including feeling the activity of one's muscles as they perform the skill. Whatever term you prefer, however, there is no question that mental rehearsal is one of the most powerful techniques for programming the body to perform as you want it to.

People in all walks of life, including many great athletes, have used imagery to enhance their performance. Moreover, research has supported the claims of many athletes that imagery improves their performance. Scientific studies have shown that although physical practice is still the most effective single method for learning and improving an athletic skill, a combination of physical *and* mental practice is often more effective than physical practice alone.

All of us have had firsthand experience in ways that our imagination can affect our thoughts, feelings, and behavior. Going back to your own childhood, can you recall instances in which you experienced excitement by thinking about the gift you might receive for your birthday or Christmas? Can you recall an instance in which you experienced the "dreads" by anticipating something very bad that might happen to you? Can you remember imitating the skills and style of your sport heroes? In all of these instances, imagery was involved. To imitate a baseball hero, for example, you had to be able to imagine his batting stance, how he swung the bat, how he wound up and threw the pitch, or how he fielded his position, before you could copy it. Perhaps you even put yourself in his place, performing the same actions on a big league field situated in your mind.

Imagery training can be used as a means of learning or perfecting a skill, preparing oneself for competition, maintaining one's skill level while recovering from an injury, or developing a "game plan." Before describing how you can use this powerful tool to enhance your coaching effectiveness, let us consider the nature of imagery and how it works.

How Imagery Improves Performance

How does imagery work? How can simply imagining an action lead to an actual improvement in performance? The answer is that when we learn or perfect a skill, tiny electrical circuits are established in the nervous system and in the muscles that perform the act. Thus, when athletes engage in sport movements, the brain is constantly transmitting impulses to the muscles for the production of the movements. The reason imagery works is that similar impulses occur in the brain and muscles when athletes imagine the movements without actually performing them. Electrical recordings from the brain and muscles suggest that the low-level firing of nerve and muscle cells creates in the nervous system and muscles a kind of blueprint to help the individual execute the movement later on. This is sometimes called "muscle memory."

Whether athletes actually perform movements or whether they simply imagine performing them, performance circuits in the brain and muscles are activated and strengthened with repetition. Imagery may have special benefits for strengthening the performance blueprint. Research in the former Soviet Union and at the University of Washington has shown that a mixture of mental rehearsal and physical practice actually results in a higher level of subsequent performance on athletic tasks than does 100% physical practice.

We know that imagery is effective for older athletes, but what about children? Actually there is reason to expect that it might be even *more* effective for children. Children tend to be more image-oriented in their thinking than are adults, whose thinking tends to be more verbal in nature. In other words, youngsters tend to have more active and vivid imaginations. Studies of hypnotizability have shown that children tend to have greater ability than many adults to "get into" the suggestions (many of which involve imagery, such as imagining that one's hand is getting heavier and can't be moved).

Sport psychologists are now capitalizing on these imaginal abilities of children, and the first studies of imagery training with young athletes are appearing in the scientific literature. In one such study, carried out by Dr. Li-Wie Zhang and his coworkers, 7- to 10-year-old elite Chinese table tennis players watched videotapes of the world's best players and imagined themselves performing the same techniques for 6 minutes a day three times a week for 16 weeks. These children showed much larger performance gains than did equally skilled children who

Key Principle

Recent research has shown that child athletes can profit significantly from mental rehearsal of sport skills.

only watched the videotapes but did not practice imagery.

You do not have to be a sport psychologist to use imagery techniques with your young athletes. By introducing them to the powers of their mind's eye, you can teach them a performance enhancement approach that they can apply in virtually any area of their life.

Introducing the Power of Imagery to Athletes

Youngsters want to be physically active when they come to practice, so you have to demonstrate the importance of imagery and justify your use of it early on. Here's a fun demonstration that shows how imagining a movement can actually cause it to occur "involuntarily."

Seat the athletes in a circle facing a bench. Seat several youngsters (chosen because they will take their task seriously) on the bench and hand each subject a 6-inch piece of string with a large paper clip attached to the end. The string should be held with the thumb and forefinger, with the elbow resting on the athlete's thigh so that the paper clip hangs like a pendulum between the knees. Tell the other children to watch but to keep silent during the demonstration.

Tell the subjects that you would like them to keep their eyes closed and to imagine the string and paper clip as vividly as they can. Ask them to nod when they form a good image of the string. Then tell them to imagine that the paper clip is beginning to move slowly back and forth, from right to left. Tell them to continue to imagine that it swings back and forth, more and more. After awhile you will observe that the paper clips actually begin to move, at least for some of the children. (When that happens, motion to the other children to remain silent.) Then, suggest a new image: that the paper clip is now moving toward and away from the subject. You will find that this typically occurs as well. You can also suggest clockwise or counterclockwise circular movements. (When the other athletes observe what happens, they will want to try the demonstration, too. You might want to arrange some time after practice for this so as to conserve time and maintain control over the proceedings.)

After the demonstration (which generally works for the majority of the children), you can introduce the idea that imagining and "feeling" a skill helps one to perform it better. Tell them that many champion athletes use imagery regularly, and that they can use it, too.

Incorporating Imagery Training into Your Practices

Many coaches of high school, college, and professional athletes schedule a 10- to 15-minute imagery period into their practice sessions, during which athletes form vivid images of performing sports skills flawlessly or mentally preparing themselves for the situations they expect to encounter. With younger athletes, imagery sessions exceeding 5 minutes can tax the athletes' attention span. Thus you need to have your imagery session well planned. A good time to do imagery is immediately after stretching or warm-ups.

> **Key Principle**
>
> In order to profit from imagery training, the athlete must have the coach's guidance on exactly what to imagine and "feel."

In developing and refining skills through imagery, the athlete must know precisely what to imagine or rehearse, and then must form images that involve not only visual images, but also images of what the movements *feel like* in the muscles. In order to form the correct image, the athlete must have a model for what to do. This can be based on watching someone else perform the activity or on the athlete's memory of a correct performance in the past.

When athletes are learning a new skill, most coaches show them how to do the particular skill. For example, baseball coaches show and tell the athletes how the bat should be swung, how the glove should be positioned to catch the ball, or which base the ball should be thrown to. Sometimes they have athletes who have already mastered the skill demonstrate it, or they show pictures or videotapes depicting the skill. Any of these demonstrations can be the basis for imagery. After the skill is demonstrated, tell the athletes to close their eyes and to see and feel themselves performing the skill, emphasizing the specific elements they should focus on. At first you can have them view themselves "from the outside," as if they were watching a videotape of themselves. Then they should imagine it "from the inside," as they would actually experience it. Emphasize the importance of trying to "feel" the action as well as seeing it in their imagination. Have them imagine performing the activity four to five times. You can use other embellishments, such as seeing the action in slow motion. The main thing is that they get engaged in the imagery.

For strategic instruction, such as playing a particular defense or reacting to a specific game situation, discuss with the athletes exactly what should be done, making sure that each knows his or her assignment. Then have the athletes imagine themselves react in the desired way.

After the athletes have done the imagery, have them perform the actual skill and to notice any differences between what they imagined (presumably, the correct way to perform the act) and their actual behavior. This can provide valuable information on which specific elements of the skill or strategy need more work in both imagery and action. This approach also helps train your athletes to problem-solve and make adjustments, a valuable life skill.

The beauty of mental rehearsal is that it can occur anywhere. Thus, a young athlete can shoot 20 free throws or block 20 shots on goal in the mental arena of the mind. Once a particular image has been established, encourage your athletes to spend a few minutes doing the imagery on their own. You (and they) will be surprised at the extent to which this process can speed up skill development. You can work with each individual athlete within the goal-setting concepts described in Chapter 5 and decide which skills should be the focus of imagery training.

Key Principle
Encourage your athletes to practice imagery on their own, both to refine skills and to prepare themselves for competition.

The positive approach emphasized throughout the book applies to imagery as well as to coaching behaviors and goal setting. Images should always focus on the desired response, never on the undesired one. The reason is obvious: imagining what one does *not* want to do actually programs the body to do just that. Caution your athletes to always form positive images, and make sure your instructions during imagery do not contain "don't" elements. To experience why, see what happens when we tell you *not* to imagine a pink elephant right now. What image did you form?

Mental Preparation for Competition

As Nolan Ryan did, many elite athletes use mental imagery to prepare for competition. Encourage your young athletes to do the same. A few minutes before each competition, meet with your athletes and give them any last-minute instructions or reminders. Then, have them close their eyes and relax by focusing on their breathing and mentally saying "Relax" to themselves as they exhale. After perhaps 30 seconds of relaxation, ask them to vividly imagine and feel what it will be like to perform the specific skills or strategies you have just discussed. This can help relax and focus your athletes on what you want them to do.

Encourage your young athletes to use imagery to prepare themselves for competition even before they come to the competitive site. These few minutes of imagery can pay dividends in terms of mental preparation for competition.

Finally, encourage your athletes to use imagery in other areas of their life as well. Imagery, used correctly, is a life skill that can enhance performance in school, in social and family situations, and in peer relationships. Skills can be refined and valuable planning can occur in the mind's eye.

Part 4

Health and Safety Considerations

Physical Development

An athlete's body greatly affects his or her athletic potential and has much to do with the enjoyment and satisfaction that comes from training and competition. What are the features of body structure that affect sport participation? Height is an obviously important characteristic. There is always one 5-foot, 8-inch guard in a high school basketball tournament, but given equal ability, the 6-foot, 6-inch player has a better chance of scoring more points. Weight is another aspect of body size that determines potential success. The 200-pound football player has a distinct playing advantage over an opponent who weighs only two-thirds as much.

Body build, or physique, must also be considered. The three major body types (somatotypes) are described as follows:

- Endomorphs are characterized by a soft roundness throughout the body, with a tendency toward fatness.

- Mesomorphs are muscular individuals with large, prominent bones.

- Ectomorphs have thin body segments and poor muscle development.

Successful athletes in a particular sport tend to have similar body builds, and their physiques are compatible with the requirements of the activity. Being a mesomorph or an ectomorph will have a lot to do with whether an individual must be satisfied with recreational jogging or will enjoy working his or her long, thin legs in competitive distance races. But having a certain body type does not guarantee success or failure. The outcome is not absolute. With this in mind, you can help youngsters to select sports that are in harmony with their body build. This will give them a better chance to achieve higher levels of performance.

In addition to body size and build, athletic performance is influenced by body composition—the relative amounts of bone, muscle, and fat that make up body mass. The role of muscle in moving the body and generating force is of prime importance. Quite simply, the more strength and power that an athlete has, the greater his or her advantage will be. On the other hand, fatty tissue represents excess baggage and is a performance-inhibitor. Fatness reduces speed, limits endurance and, in some sports, increases the risk of injury. In almost all sports, with the exception of sumo wrestling perhaps, elite athletes strive to be trim and muscular, with healthy minimal levels of body fat.

Key Principle

Body structure and function are important in determining how satisfying and enjoyable sports can be.

The physical characteristics that determine sport performance are constantly changing during the growing years of childhood and adolescence. When coaches are knowledgeable about the nature and extent of growth, they are better able to answer crucial questions about *what sport for what child at what age*. Moreover, such information makes it is possible to project realistic expectations of sport performance on youngsters and to direct training programs that their changing bodies will respond to. As boys and girls move through the exciting stages of growing up in sport, some appreciation of the ever-changing body can make the experience the satisfying one it should be.

Factors That Influence Body Characteristics

With the exception of identical twins, no two human bodies are exactly the same. Body size, shape, and composition, as well as the body's million physiological characteristics, are unique to each individual. These physical traits are influenced by age and sex, along with a host of internal and external (environmental) factors. For example, the endocrine glands secrete hormones directly into the bloodstream. Hormones are basically regulators of body functions, and they play an important role in physical growth and sexual maturation. With respect to environmental forces, body structure and function depend on how adequate nutrition has been, how free from disease the body has been, and how physically active one has been.

Most importantly, body characteristics are influenced by genetic factors. Certainly we know that parent height is related to offspring height. Hereditary influences on body structure and its many functions are so important in determining the potential for athletic performance that it is often said that great athletes are born, not made. The significance of one's genetic endowment cannot be denied.

Aside from the size, shape, and makeup of the body, several ways in which body functions respond to exercise and training are important contributors to athletic performance. As with the body's structure, these abilities to respond to training are in large part determined by genetic characteristics. They include: (a) the potential for developing outstanding muscle strength, (b) the capability of producing muscle energy efficiently, and (c) the capability of increasing the body's metabolism to a very high level to meet the demands of vigorous exercise. Quick reaction and speed of movement are also important to the athlete, as are the potentials for speed and quickness. These traits are all inheritable.

We've emphasized that hereditary factors are critical in determining which children can look forward to being outstanding, and perhaps even elite, athletes. However, the effects of genetics are never absolute, because genes do not operate in isolation. We cannot undervalue the influence of the environments in which we live—natural, social, and athletic. During childhood and adolescence, regular exercise is among the many environmental factors essential to achieve full potential for growth. Moderate physical stress from the muscle activities found in most sports is generally a positive force on bone growth. Yet it is doubtful whether training programs for young athletes have any growth-promoting

Key Principle

If someone wishes to develop the body of an elite athlete and the potential to respond ideally to a sport training program, the individual should select his or her parents with great care.

effect on their height. Dramatic exercise effects do, however, occur in muscle and adipose (fat) tissue. Following the start of adolescence in males, the increase in muscle mass is directly related to the intensity and duration of training programs. And, of course, the loss of fatty tissue from exercise is a desirable effect of sport participation.

On the side of caution, relatively little is known about the limits beyond which strenuous physical activity can be harmful to a young athlete's growth. Unfortunately, there is no exact guide for determining how much activity is appropriate. Important factors include the maturation level of the child and the frequency and duration of the activity. The most reasonable approach is to rely on the child's own tolerance. The young athlete will generally know when his or her limit has been reached.

A related and equally important issue concerns the exercise tolerance of healthy children. Do endurance sports place *excessive* demands on the hearts of young athletes? No. This is a popular myth. There is increasing evidence that the growing child's heart responds favorably to the normal levels of physical exertion in such sports.

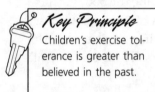

Key Principle

Children's exercise tolerance is greater than believed in the past.

The key to safely handling the demands of heavy exercise resides in the health of the child. This points to the need for careful medical screening, which includes probing for a family history of cardiac problems and any early cardiovascular difficulties. Also, in protecting the wellness of child athletes, competent coaches play a critical role in supervising appropriate endurance-training procedures.

Patterns of Physical Growth

There is an abundance of information concerning the growth of American children. Growth can be looked at merely as heights or weights for given ages, as seen in Figure 8.1. This curve indicates a child's growth status, or the size attained at a particular age.

It is interesting to look at the increases in height and weight that occur during a given period of time. The curve shown in Figure 8.2 illustrates the rate of growth, that is, centimeters or kilograms gained

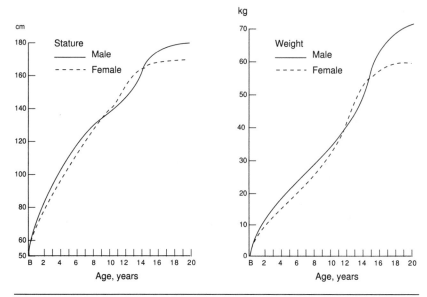

Figure 8.1 *Typical growth in height and weight for boys and girls. For height, 2.54 cm = 1 inch; for weight, 1 kg = 2.20 pounds.*

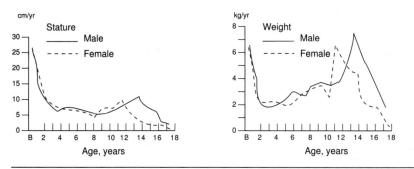

Figure 8.2 *Changing rates of height and weight increases for boys and girls.*

per year. We can see that the most rapid period of growth occurs immediately after birth, and then the growth rate slows to a modest, steady process during childhood. This is followed by an adolescent growth spurt and then by deceleration until growth finally stops. There is little difference in the relative growth rates of boys and girls during childhood. However, as shown in Figure 8.1, during childhood boys are slightly taller and heavier than girls of the same age. This difference is a relatively minor one and of no real practical significance for sport performance.

When girls experience the rapid growth spurt that occurs between the ages of 10.5 and 13, they become taller than boys. During pubescence tall girls will be taller than tall boys, and all girls will be taller than the shortest 3 to 5% of boys. This is a temporary situation that changes when boys begin to experience their adolescent growth spurt in height some 2 years after girls have experienced their peak velocity in gaining height.

Prior to adolescence, sex differences in body composition are minor. However, boys do have slightly more bone and muscle tissue and less fat than girls. Following the period of maximum gain in height that occurs in early adolescence (about age 12 to 13 for girls and 14 to 15 for boys), there is a period of maximum gain in weight. In girls this is due primarily to a large increase in body fat, with a relatively small increase in muscle tissue. In boys the rapid gain in body weight that follows a rapid gain in height is due to a decrease in relative body fatness and a striking increase in muscle mass. Consequently, postadolescent girls have only about two thirds as much muscle as males, and young adult females have almost twice the amount of body fat.

Key Principle

Girls are nearer their final body size at any age because they mature at a faster rate than boys.

Because boys, on the average, begin their rapid gain in height at the age of 12.5, they have about 2 more years of preadolescent growth than girls have. During this 2-year period they continue to grow, and at age 14 or 15 they are about 4 inches taller than girls were when they began their rapid growth. In the immediate preadolescent period, boys' legs grow much faster than their trunks. Thus, the longer period of preadolescent growth for males is responsible for the fact that legs of adult males are longer than those of females.

Key Principle

All boys and girls experience an adolescent growth spurt.

The age at which the adolescent growth spurt begins varies widely from one individual to another. The variation is so great in a sample of normal males, for example, that some boys may have their most rapid growth as early as their twelfth birthday, whereas others will not have this growth experience until they are nearly 16. These slower-maturing boys will not have their muscle growth and rapid gain in body weight until more than 14 months later, at 17 or 18 years of age. A very normal but slowly maturing young male will have completed high school before he is physically suited to compete in many sports requiring large size, strength, and a mature skeleton.

The differences in age at which adolescent growth and physical development occur are most evident during junior high school or middle school, or at 12 to 15 years of age. Normal boys can vary as much as 15 inches in height, 90 pounds in weight, and 5 years in maturation status, that is, biologic age. (Biologic age is commonly determined by an X-ray examination of skeletal maturation.) Most youth sport programs match competitors on the basis of calendar age. Therefore, large numbers of boys, who do not experience their growth and maturation close to the average, risk some very significant problems. This is true for both the slow later maturer and the advanced early maturer. We will discuss these specific concerns later in the chapter.

Changes in Physical Abilities During Childhood and Adolescence

During the childhood years, as boys and girls grow—resulting in longer arms and legs and increased muscle tissue—both have the potential to increase their strength. Boys and girls show similar increased ability to perform motor skills prior to puberty. However, in general, boys are eventually able to develop greater strength and thus surpass girls in the performance of most sport-related skills.

During adolescence males show a steady increase in performance and endurance that extends into early adulthood. The same is not true for girls. There has been a tendency for girls' performance to reach a plateau around the time of puberty (approximately 13 years of age) and decline thereafter. Because of physical changes that accompany adolescence, such as increases in fat, girls are placed at somewhat of a disadvantage for motor performance. But the leveling off and subsequent decline in girls' performance and endurance have been related more to social factors than to biological changes.

Key Principle

For adolescent females, decreased motivation and increased sedentary habits are major causes of lowered performance.

Like other aspects of motor skill, strength shows a steady increase during childhood, with boys being slightly stronger than girls. Boys continue to improve during adolescence, whereas girls' strength scores level off and then tend to decrease. In boys there is a delay, on the average, of at least 14 months between the period of the most rapid gain in height and the most rapid gain in muscle weight. The adolescent male who is nearing the completion of his rapid gain in height will have little muscle tissue and strength potential for the next year or two. He must await the development of muscles to go along with his newly acquired taller body. Thus, the adolescent male is not as strong as his stature might suggest.

This lag in strength was apparent in a 7-foot, 2-inch college basketball freshman who had not yet begun his muscle maturation and weight gain. At 7-2 he weighed only 172 pounds. When he suffered a muscle strain, his coach remarked, "This is good news and bad news. The bad news is that he is going to miss practice for several days. The good news is that now we know he has a muscle!"

For many years, it was believed that prepubescents could not significantly improve their strength as a result of weight training. This was attributed to insufficient amounts of muscle-building hormones (androgens) in the bloodstream prior to puberty. In recent years, however, research has well documented that prepubescent boys and girls can indeed achieve measurable increases in strength. In studies conducted over 8 to 14 weeks of training with hydraulic resistance equipment, weight machines, and free weights, strength-trained subjects increased strength by 22 to 74% in various tests, compared with 3 to 14% for nonstrength-trained subjects. Such increases before puberty may be more the result neuromuscular adaptation (motor learning) than muscular adaptation (hypertrophy). In other words, prepubescent youngsters may gain strength by learning to use their muscles more effectively through practice.

Because the increase in weight of the adolescent female is due primarily to a gain in fat (and, to only a small extent, to a gain in muscle tissue), her potential for strength development via exercise is much less than the male's. In young adult women, weight training has been shown to produce significant gains in strength, but in the absence of male hormones (androgens), the female will experience less marked gains in the size and mass of muscles.

Should Boys and Girls Compete Against Each Other?

We have pointed out that during childhood years, only very slight sex differences in body structure and motor performance are present. On a purely physical basis, there is no reason why prepubescent boys and girls should not be on the same teams competing with and against each other. The levels of performance and the chances for causing or sustaining injury do not differ significantly between the two sexes during childhood.

> **Key Principle**
> After puberty, girls should have separate but equal opportunities for sport participation.

The situation changes drastically during adolescence. As boys gain more in height, weight, muscle mass, and strength, it is not possible for girls to *fairly* and *safely* compete against them in most sports. After age 11, boys and girls should have their own competitive opportunities in those sports in which strength and body size are determinants of proficiency and injury risk.

The Growing and Maturing Skeleton

The body skeleton is obviously involved in the normal growth of children. In adolescents the skeleton first grows in size and length, after which it gains in density and strength. As mentioned above, the principal sites of growth before the start of rapid adolescent growth are in the legs and arms. During the adolescent growth spurt, the trunk grows most rapidly. The long bones of the arms and legs increase their length by the activity of specialized cells located in a so-called growth plate at either end of the shaft of the long bones.

Because it is composed of cartilage (soft tissue), the growth plate is structurally the weakest point in the bone. It is weaker than any point in the shaft of the bone and actually weaker than the ligaments that align the neighboring joints. Additionally, the growth plate is weakest during periods of most rapid growth. Injury to this area of the bone can destroy those cells responsible for the future growth of the long bone. During the period of the most rapid gain in height (on the average, ages 14 to 15 in boys and 12 to 13 in girls), severe injury to the ends of long bones can threaten the growth plate. Growth arrest and a shortened leg could result in lifelong crippling if a long bone of the leg is involved.

Fortunately, growth-plate injuries are not common in sports. But the threat of a growth-plate injury is a major concern in collision sports, such as football and wrestling, where severe blows to a leg or arm may be encountered. As the skeleton matures, the bones become denser, stronger, and more able to withstand the trauma of hard use in intensive training. Finally, as growth nears completion in later adolescence, the growth plate ceases its function, fuses firmly with the shaft of the long bone, and is no longer the site of vulnerability that it was during early adolescence.

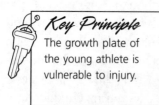

Key Principle
The growth plate of the young athlete is vulnerable to injury.

Sport Participation and Physical Maturity

We have mentioned that body structure and a variety of basic functions that relate to athletic performance undergo striking change during the early years of adolescence. And there is great variation in the age at which individuals experience these changes. Therefore, the age at which children (boys in particular) are physically ready for many types of sports will also vary greatly. Youth sport programs present the early adolescent (junior high or middle school-aged person) with opportunities for highly organized sports. It thus becomes important to identify early-maturing and late-maturing individuals if they are to be directed into appropriate sport experiences. The late maturer will have increased risk of injury, with his undeveloped muscles and immature skeleton. More importantly, playing with and competing against larger, stronger, and more mature boys, the late maturer will be a less-skilled athlete. He is a prime candidate to drop out at the earliest opportunity.

The considerable variation in the onset of physical development at adolescence raises the question of the appropriateness of collision sports for junior high school and middle school boys. After one junior high school football game, 22 players were weighed. They varied in weight from 84 to 212 pounds. Although the players' physical maturity was not scientifically assessed, the range of maturity seemed also to be extremely varied—as much as 4 or 5 years' variation in skeletal maturity. Unless steps are taken to match competitors on the basis of maturity and size in football, wrestling, and ice hockey, it is difficult to justify these sports for middle and junior high school programs.

The Early Maturer

The early-maturing individual is bigger, stronger, and quicker, acquires sport skills faster, and has more endurance potential than his peers. Thus, the early-maturing boy can be expected to be a star grade school and junior high school athlete.

That early-maturing boys excel in several juvenile athletic programs has been well documented. In football and track-and-field events, early maturity has been shown to be a prime determinant of proficiency. Players at the Little League World Series have been studied using bone-age X-rays to document their maturation status. In one report, 71% of these 12-year-old star athletes had advanced bone ages. Those with the most advanced bone age were pitchers, first basemen, left fielders, and those who batted fourth (clean-up) in the batting order. In one World Series, the winning pitcher in the championship game was a very mature 5-foot, 8-inch, 174-pound 12-year-old.

Key Principle
The difference in ability level of young athletes is often a result of different maturity levels.

A major problem is that the early maturer enjoys outstanding sport success during elementary, middle, and early junior high school simply because of the physical advantages he has over his teammates and opponents. With the elaborate sport programs available for very young athletes in most communities, the 8- to 12-year-old can readily become a true sports star. That winning Little League pitcher mentioned above was flown to New York from the West Coast to appear on a national prime-time television show, and he was given a page and a half write-up in *Sports Illustrated*. A local television commentator suggested that the junior high school where he had just started seventh grade be named after him. Pretty heady stuff for a 12-year-old.

The sport success of an early-maturing boy can lead to a full-time commitment to one or more sports at a very early age. Sport achievements may eliminate the desire for accomplishment in other areas, such as school work or the arts, or an interest in exploring other sports. Positive feedback comes from coaches, teammates, and most particularly parents, who sometimes begin to think of their star athlete in terms of outstanding high school performances, college scholarships, and perhaps even a high-salaried career in professional sports.

The world can fall apart for this youngster about high school time, when as a sophomore he lines up against some juniors and seniors who possess his same maturity. Having lost the advantage of his early development, the young man is now less than an outstanding athlete. As all of his former grade school teammates and opponents catch up to him in maturity and as other athletes begin to do outstanding things, the grade school star may find only an uncomfortable place on the bench. Unable to understand the true reason that the star no longer outshines others, insensitive coaches may accuse him of "dogging it." The young man has lost the limelight of sport success on which his self-esteem was built. He is left with no other interests or talents because of his early all-consuming commitment to the sport, and he is keenly aware that others view him as a great disappointment. At 16 or 17, an age of considerable vulnerability to a number of disturbing antisocial alternatives, he is a depressed has-been.

The answer, of course, is to prevent the problems from occurring. This can be done by first recognizing the signs of early maturity. The early maturer will probably be the son of a father who likewise was an early maturer, and he will experience growth changes and sexual maturation well ahead of schedule. Once identified as an individual who is maturing more rapidly than usual, he should have the opportunity to participate in sports with individuals who are of similar maturity, not the same calendar age. The early-maturing star basketball player of junior high school should have a chance to work out with the high school junior varsity. Matches can be arranged for the 12-year-

Key Principle

The potential problems of early maturing athletes are fairly easy to avoid.

old tennis star with some 16-year-old members at the tennis club. Early-maturing boys need to know how really good they are if they are to keep their athletic performances and potentials in proper perspective.

The Late Maturer

With sport successes so closely related to maturity, it isn't difficult to imagine the problems of the late-maturing boy. Many, but certainly not all, late maturers will be small in stature for their age. They will have less strength, endurance, and skeletal maturity and lower motor skills than their average peers. These boys are going to be handicapped in many sports where size, strength, and endurance determine the outcome, and in some situations they will be at undue risk to injury.

The late-maturing individual will often be recognized as such in his elementary school years. And, as true for the early maturer, a father's maturation experience can be an indicator of the maturation rate to be expected of the son. If early sport participation is important for the late maturer, he should be directed to sports that are not primarily dependent on size and strength for proficiency, such as racket sports, diving, and some track events. He may not become state champion, but he may achieve levels of accomplishment sufficient to earn him a comfortable place in the sport scene.

Many late maturers can comfortably postpone their entry into sport programs until they are physically mature. Club activities, scouting, music, and other activities may satisfy in the meanwhile. It is most important that these boys know the normal sequence of changes that occur during adolescence so that they know where they are in the maturation process, where they are going, and when they get there. With this insight they will know when sports can be rewarding, when a vigorous training program can be effective and satisfying, and when they can be competitive on the field or court. It is possible at ages 14 to 16 to avoid a devastating, negative sport experience due to delayed maturity. The late maturer doesn't have to suffer consistent setbacks and be turned off to sports and their benefits.

Key Principle
Late-maturing youngsters need understanding and special attention from coaches and parents alike.

Coaches and parents should know the implications of delayed adolescent development in these boys, and they should develop their expectations accordingly. Limited training for strength and endurance during the first two years of high school should be accompanied by large doses of encouragement on the court or field and at home. Properly managed, the late maturer can be a budding sport star by the senior year of high school. Being constantly yelled at by a coach or put down by a disappointed parent can produce a demoralized dropout at an age when dropping out can be very serious.

The Body of Today's Young Athlete

Those responsible for youth sport programs must recognize that athletes are a different population from those of a generation or two ago. Athletes today are bigger and stronger at younger ages. Particularly at the junior and senior high school levels, the "new model" athletes not only perform better, they demand a higher degree of sophistication and concern in dealing with their protective equipment, training facilities, coaching, officiating, and even rule changes.

> *Key Principle*
> Children are growing to a larger size and maturing more rapidly than ever before.

The young athlete's body is the prime determinant of proficiency and satisfaction in sports. Since physical features are constantly changing during childhood and adolescence, sport programs and expectations must be adjusted according to these developmental changes. From a purely physical viewpoint, the sport programs of elementary school children must minimize demands for strength and endurance. Prior to the age of 12 or 13, sports should be for fun and for acquiring proficiency in a wide variety of fundamental motor skills.

During those rapidly changing years from 12 to 16, with their tremendous variation in adolescent body changes, more attention should be paid to the proper matching of competitors. Young athletes should ideally be of a similar maturational level regardless of their calendar ages. Sports provide a critical opportunity to acquire much-needed confidence in oneself and in one's newly developed physique. The adolescent should not be denied this opportunity or have a negative experience because of inappropriate matching or unrealistic performance expectations.

Training and Conditioning

Conditioning, or getting in shape, is as much a part of sport as the competition itself. In addition to the concerns of the elite performer, the recreational athlete is becoming increasingly aware of the importance of good conditioning practices simply to stay fit, feel better, and enjoy his or her hours of sport. For the young athlete, a proper introduction to the need for and the techniques of good conditioning is essential to a good beginning.

Today's champion athletes are establishing new world records every year by taking advantage of conditioning methods developed in modern exercise science laboratories. Scientists have developed practical measures of fitness and have identified components of effective conditioning programs. Such conditioning programs are useful not only for the world-class athlete preparing for competition but also for the casual recreational athlete or the individual who simply wants to take care of his or her body and enjoy feeling fit.

Exercise scientists have identified five components of a comprehensive conditioning program. These are body composition, flexibility, strength and power, endurance, and speed.

> **Key Principle**
>
> A proper conditioning program is necessary to enjoying sports, and it is a keystone in lifelong fitness and good health.

Shaping Up for Competition

Body Composition

Certain levels of body fatness are associated with elite performance in various popular sports, with certain positions on some teams, and with different events in track and field. Body fatness can be estimated by measuring skin fat folds. The result is expressed as the percentage of body weight that is estimated to be made up of body fat.

The levels of fatness listed in Table 9.1 provide general goals for early preseason conditioning. Commonly, it is necessary to reduce body fat to the desired level. The fatness levels listed in the table are for elite athletes and are consistent with the finest levels of health and fitness—when these levels are reached in a proper manner. The following points pertain to a program of fatness reduction compatible with good health and effective training:

- Allow plenty of time to reduce body fat. Decrease body-fat weight at a rate no more rapid than 2 or 3 pounds each week.

- Calculate a specific goal of fatness level and determine what the body weight will be when that fatness level is achieved. This weight should be the athlete's stable competing weight, which should be constant throughout the sport season.

In addition to a vigorous exercise routine, a modest reduction in food intake is essential during the period of fatness reduction. The diet during this period of early preseason conditioning should be no less than approximately 2,000 kilocalories per day for a typical high school or college-aged athlete.

For the junior high school male who wishes to control his level of fatness for sport participation, his energy intake should also be no less than 2,000 kilocalories, if growth is to continue at a normal rate. For many chubby but rapidly growing junior high school students who are just beginning to play sports seriously, it is often a good policy to maintain a stationary weight through a program of conditioning exercises and a controlled diet.

> **Key Principle**
> Reducing body fat demands increasing training, which requires the expenditure of a significant amount of energy.

Table 9.1

Relative Body-Fat Values for Elite Male and Female Athletes in Various Sports*

Sport	Males Fat (%)	Females Fat (%)
Baseball/softball	12–14	16–26
Basketball	7–10	16–27
Football	8–18	—
Gymnastics	4–6	9–15
Ice hockey	13–15	—
Jockeys	12–15	—
Skiing	7–14	18–20
Soccer	9–12	—
Speed skating	10–12	—
Swimming	5–10	14–16
Track and field		
Sprinters	6–9	8–20
Middle distance runners	6–12	8–16
Distance runners	4–8	6–12
Discus	14–18	16–24
Shot put	14–18	20–30
Jumpers and hurdlers	6–9	8–16
Tennis	14–16	18–22
Volleyball	8–14	16–26
Weight lifting	8–16	—
Wrestling	4–12	—

* The values represent the range of means reported in various published and unpublished studies.

Following this policy enables youngsters to continue their rapid growth and outgrow their moderate fatness. Modest increases in body fat normally occur in boys immediately before they experience the rapid linear growth of early adolescence. This is merely Nature's way of providing some stored energy in anticipation of the great nutrition demands of the adolescent growth spurt. It is a normal increase in fat and is not an indication that he is destined to be an overly fat adolescent during junior and senior high school years.

It is helpful in every conditioning program to make a decision as to the goals of the program and how intensely involved a given individual will become in it. The highly competitive scholastic or collegiate athlete will be satisfied with nothing less than the ideal body composition for a particular sport. The young preadolescent on the soccer team, for example, may make less of a commitment to fitness. Conditioning for such young athletes may be confined to regular energy-expending exercise, a good mixed diet, and enjoyable, regular sport participation. Their goal should be to maintain a normal body fatness level of 12 to 14% rather than the very trim 6 to 8% of the elite population of professional soccer players.

Exercise involving regular expenditures of energy is the first essential to fatness control for everyone, including the obese preadolescent. At this age, the fat level is controlled for health and fitness, not to develop elite athletic skills in some sport. Maintaining a desired body composition should also be seen by the 10- to 12-year-old girl or boy as important to health and fitness—not just to make him or her a better athlete.

> **Key Principle**
>
> Paying attention to fatness level is a sound part of the conditioning program of all individuals regardless of sex or age.

An early conditioning program has the potential to alter body composition by increasing body muscle mass. Large numbers of adolescent males are interested in increasing their body weight to improve their playing potential in high school or community-based sport programs. Football is an obvious example of a very popular sport that gives a premium in performance to heavier, stronger individuals. Many young men attempt to increase their body weight by eating more to become more proficient football players. It should be emphasized, however, that only muscle work will increase muscle weight and size. Thus, the young man who wants to increase his playing potential by increasing his muscle weight will have to become involved in a regular weight training program. In addition, the young man should record all the food eaten in a weight-maintenance diet so that he can document a daily increase of 700 to 800 kilocalories of any preferred foods. Here again, planning ahead is essential. The maximum weight gain in lean body tissues—muscle—is about 1 to 2 pounds per week. The weight training por-

> **Key Principle**
>
> Achieving and controlling a desired body composition through a well-planned preseason conditioning program can provide one of the greatest health benefits of athletic participation.

tion of any conditioning program should be carefully supervised. It should involve all of the body's large muscle groups.

For females, both before and after the onset of puberty, weight training will result in strength gains; but as noted in Chapter 8, it will have relatively little effect in increasing muscle mass. Women who are well into the changes of adolescence or older will also experience some increase in muscle strength from a weight training program. But again, it will be much less than in the male, even with the same effort. Finally, it is well known that there will be considerable individual variation in the response of young women to weight training.

Flexibility

The serious young athlete and the active recreational-sport participant will both benefit from developing joint flexibility and fluidity of motion. Good flexibility may reduce some of the risk of muscle and tendon injuries in vigorous exercise and competition. It can reduce soreness and stiffness after exercise, and it is conducive to that fluidity of motion that is seen in very talented and so-called natural athletes. Stretching exercises and improved joint mobility are important for all athletes, but participants in some sports are more dependent on good flexibility than others. The high hurdler must have a high degree of flexibility, the swimmer must have well developed ankle and shoulder flexibility, and those in various running events in track competition derive particular benefit from flexibility exercises, since they may develop very tight muscles from the tremendous amount of running during their training.

Muscles can be stretched and flexibility gained by holding a muscle in a stretched position for several seconds. The static flexibility exercises described below are designed to stretch each of the major muscle groups. These maneuvers provide a good general stretching program. Certain sports and the use of specific muscle groups may demand stretching other specific muscle groups.

In the exercises that follow, static stretching is done by slowly lengthening the muscle until the first signs of real pull, or

Key Principle
Flexibility may decrease the risk of injury and it does improve performance.

tightness. The position is held for 5 to 10 seconds. Then the stretch is slowly released as one assumes the original starting position. It is ill-advised to bounce, jerk, or painfully force the stretch. Tightness, soreness, and small muscle tears can result, and these are counterproductive to the goals of fluidity and flexibility of motion that one is trying to achieve. A good flexibility-maintenance routine is the following, to which stretches for a particular sport can be added.

1. *Trunk rotation.* With hands on the hips and the feet shoulder width apart, twist to the left as far as possible and then twist to the right as far as you can.

2. *Shoulder rotation.* Extend one arm and rotate it completely around in the largest possible circle. Do each arm separately, first forward and then in the opposite direction.

3. *Side stretch.* Spread the feet about 3 feet apart, put your hands behind your head, and keep your legs straight. Now lean sideways until you begin to feel the muscles pull along the side of the trunk.

4. *Hamstring stretch.* With the feet together and the legs straight at the knee, lean forward until you feel, in the large muscles in the back of the upper leg, a sensation of pulling. Hold the position for 5 to 10 seconds, and repeat.

5. *Quadriceps stretch.* Grasp your right foot behind your body with your left hand as you hold on to the edge of a table or chair for balance. Pull the right foot up toward the back of your body until you feel a pull in the large muscle mass in the front of the thigh. Hold the position for 5 seconds, and return to a standing position with both feet on the ground. Repeat the stretching procedure with the left foot and right hand, stretching the left quadriceps muscle mass on the front of the left thigh.

6. *Calf-muscle stretch.* With the left foot about 3 feet behind the right foot, both feet facing forward and flat on the ground, bend the right knee and lean forward, keeping the left heel flat on the ground. You will begin to feel a pull in the muscles in the back of the lower leg, the calf muscles. Hold the position for 5 seconds. Repeat with the feet reversed, stretching the calf muscles of the opposite lower leg.

For the active recreational athlete or the younger competitor in junior or senior high school, each of these stretching maneuvers is best repeated 10 to 12 times. Conscientious athletes will stretch out with this routine before and after each practice. Many athletic trainers and experienced athletes firmly believe that a well-followed stretching program is important in the prevention of sport injuries. Additionally, good stretching will increase motion and performance and make active participation more pleasurable, even for the very young athlete.

Strength and Power

There are few sports in which performance cannot be related to strength. The football player, the wrestler, the rower, the soccer player and the basketball player all become more competitive when they develop their muscle strength and power through appropriate conditioning practices. Thus, strength training programs are a very real part of training for almost all serious athletes. It wasn't long ago when many coaches and elite athletes feared that strength training and conditioning would make the athlete muscle-bound, with limited motion, speed, and flexibility. Scientific investigation has shown that quite the opposite is true.

> *Key Principle*
> Proper strength training actually increases flexibility and enhances speed while increasing strength and power at the same time.

Evidence of strength in sport is readily apparent to any sport observer. The football lineman who essentially picks up the 225-pound blocking back and sets him neatly out of the play is demonstrating pure strength. Muscle power, on the other hand, is the explosive strength that is applied in the briefest time period: the fraction of a second when the shot put is hurled to a new record; when the baseball pitcher puts extra speed on his fastball; or when the high jumper goes over the bar.

In addition to muscle power and muscle strength, there is a factor of muscle endurance that is influenced by conditioning and that becomes a determinant of muscle performance. The young wrestler who may be quick and strong and powerful may not do well against an opponent with less strength and power if his muscle endurance is not as great. Even in the racket sports, such as tennis, squash, and paddleball, the arm strength required to hit the ball well may not always be as important as the muscle endurance needed in long matches, in which hundreds of power-demanding shots can wear out the arm.

The techniques used to condition muscles for strength, power, and endurance can vary greatly. The strength development program presented below can be implemented without any special muscle training apparatus or weight training facilities. As a gadget-free approach, it can very effectively condition the major muscle groups for strength and endurance when pursued regularly. This simple but effective strengthening program is compatible with the proper sport goals of anyone at any age with any reasonable commitment to sports.

1. *Sit-up*. Lying on the back with the knees bent, keeping the lower back flat against the floor and the hands behind the head, curl forward, feeling the pull on the abdominal muscles. (In the past, it was common to stabilize the feet under a piece of furniture or to have a partner hold them in place. This is ill-advised because it brings into play muscles other than those of the abdominal wall and it negates the intended benefit of the exercise.) You can add effectiveness by lying in front of a chair or a bed, resting your lower legs on the upper surface as you do the exercise.

2. *Push-up*. This conventional, well-known exercise is a good one. Be sure to keep the legs straight and the fingers pointing forward while lowering the upper chest down to the ground and returning to the starting position.

3. *Stationary jump*. Leg strength and jumping ability can be improved by repeatedly doing the standing jump. From a standing position, simply swing the arms upward and jump as high as possible. Repeat.

4. *Pull-up*. Grasp a bar with the knuckles facing you, and slowly pull the body up until the chin is over the bar. Be sure not to jerk or twist the legs. Return slowly to the original hanging position. Females who have less upper-body muscle strength can substitute 15 seconds of hanging from the bar for one pull-up.

5. *Hill run*. Using either a steep hill in the neighborhood or the

rows of seats at the school gym or grandstand, run at top speed up the incline for 5 seconds. Return to the starting position and repeat.

Key Principle
In almost every high school and certainly in every metropolitan community, there are weight lifting gyms with strength conditioning programs that involve the use of elaborate and often very expensive equipment.

Dr. William Haskell—a distinguished exercise scientist from Stanford University—is an advocate of this highly effective and simple strength conditioning program. He recommends a progression of the above numbered exercises in a conditioning program for males and females (see Table 9.2). For the more committed high school athlete who is involved in a specific sport, there are special supplementary exercises to strengthen specific muscle groups.

Table 9.2

Schedule for Strength-Training Program for Females and Males

Progression	Number of Repetitions				
Females	Sit-up	Push-up	Stationary jump	Pull-up	Hill run
Level 1	1	5	9	1	4
Level 2	2	8	10	1	4
Level 3	3	11	10	1	5
Level 4	4	12	12	2	5
Level 5	5	13	13	2	6
Level 6	6	14	14	3	6
Level 7	7	15	15	3	7
Males	Sit-up	Push-up	Stationary jump	Pull-up	Hill run
Level 1	10	10	9	4	4
Level 2	15	15	10	5	4
Level 3	19	19	11	6	5
Level 4	22	22	12	7	5
Level 5	25	25	13	8	6
Level 6	28	28	14	9	6
Level 7	30	30	15	10	7

Several points warrant mention about strength training with weight apparatus:

- If weight training machines are to be used, young athletes should use them only under competent supervision.

- Effective as these machines are, if used improperly they can be dangerous and harmful, particularly to the young athlete.

- Weights and weight training machines are made for adult males. The machines don't fit children, most adolescents, and females. This adds to the risk of injury.

- The results of a good weight training program depend not on any machine but on the athlete and the effort that he or she can muster to put into the program.

- Athletes will avoid many of the risks of injury if they stay with the program regularly. Irregular, spotty participation is the surest road to injury and poor results.

- Again, particularly for preadolescents, weight training apparatus should only be used with supervision and guidance of a knowledgeable weight coach.

Endurance

The strength training program that we have just discussed will increase the number of times a muscle group can work without becoming fatigued. For example, the number of pull-ups the young athlete can do will increase with each step in his or her strength training. The endurance that the athlete must have to sustain effort such as running, swimming, or cycling is quite a different kind of endurance. It is dependent on how efficiently the athlete can extract oxygen from the air by breathing and transporting it through the cardiovascular system to the working muscles. Those sports that demand endurance of this type, that use sus-

Key Principle

The athlete's ability to extract oxygen from the air and transport it to the muscles is known as his or her aerobic capacity, and the limits of this capacity vary among individuals.

tained muscle action for a minute or more, are called aerobic (oxygen-dependent) sports.

Potential aerobic capacity is an inherited trait. Training will improve almost everyone's aerobic capacity, that is, the ability to utilize oxygen to produce muscle energy, but only to the degree determined by genes. The world-class sprinter will never be a world-class distance runner. His or her world-class energy mechanisms and muscle power for running sprints won't provide the strength and endurance needed in the distance run. The elite sprinter wasn't born to be an elite distance runner.

The capacity to use oxygen for muscle work—the aerobic capacity of the athlete—is commonly measured in the laboratory by actually measuring the amount of oxygen that is inhaled during a strenuous exercise test. Measuring how much is inhaled and how much is exhaled allows scientists to calculate the precise ability of the individual to use oxygen in energy production. By repeating such tests, researchers can document the progressive improvement in aerobic capacity that results from a training program. With a regular program of intense training, progress can be impressive, but sooner or later things reach a point where no further increases are seen. The genetically controlled limit for oxygen utilization has been reached.

To train for increases in aerobic capacity, or the endurance needed for moderate to long efforts, coaches use moderate-intensity exercises, such as distance running, prolonged swimming, or bicycle riding, over a long time period. Exercise scientists have also demonstrated that short stints of moderate- to high-intensity exercise are highly effective in increasing aerobic capacity. Such training exercises are usually more attractive to and efficient in the training schedules of most athletes. Athletes now practice repeated 3- to 5-minute bouts of exercise to generate heart rates that indicate they are working at 80 to 90% of their aerobic capacity. Reaching this level of effort may require a young athlete to train regularly 4 or more days a week for 6 weeks or more.

To determine how close to maximum aerobic capacity one is exercising and how much potential for increase there may be

Key Principle

The heart rate is a valid indicator of aerobic capacity and of how close to maximum the body is working to use oxygen.

with further training, you may simply monitor heart rates during exercises. The interested young athlete can determine his or her maximum heart rate during intense exercise, and because heart rate and oxygen uptake correspond so closely, knowing one gives us a reliable measure of the other. To determine maximum heart rate, you will need a wristwatch with a sweep-second hand, and then follow these procedures:

- Stretch and warm up very well.

- Run at a speed that you can continue for only 2 or 3 minutes.

- When you can't go any farther, slow down and count your pulse rate for 10 seconds. Counting the pulse can be most easily done using the large vessels and pulse deep in front of the neck. You will want to practice taking your pulse before your trial run. Repeat the maximal-pulse running test a few times on different days until you get a reasonably consistent result. This number of pulse beats multiplied by six will be your maximal heart rate. Pulse rate will vary in individuals during their teenage years from a high of 210 per minute to no more than 175 or 180.

> ### Key Principle
> An effective conditioning program to improve aerobic capacity involves exercising at progressively greater levels of maximum aerobic capacity for relatively brief periods of time and performing such exercise repeatedly.

To improve aerobic capacity, begin with a limited number of exercise bouts at 60 to 70% of maximum aerobic capacity, as measured by your pulse rate. Increase the number of exercise bouts and the level of intensity up to 80 or 90% of maximum pulse rate. Your aerobic capacity will become conditioned to your inherited level of maximum ability to use oxygen. Dr. William Haskell developed a guide to determine from the 10-second pulse rate the percentage of maximum aerobic capacity that different exercises produce. A progressive exercise schedule based on the concept of interval training is outlined in Table 9.3. Doing the exercises three or four times each week will result in progressive improvement in aerobic capacity, and two or three aerobic workouts each week will be enough to generally maintain a given level.

Table 9.3
Ten-Second Heart Rates: Percentage of Maximum

Maximum Heart Rate

Beats per minute		Beats per 10 seconds	
204–209	25–27	27–29	29–31
198–203	24–26	26–28	28–30
192–197	23–25	25–27	27–29
186–191	23–24	24–25	25–26
180–185	22–23	23–24	24–25
%Maximum	**60–70%**	**70–80%**	**80–90%**

Aerobic Training Schedule, Running or Swimming

Level	Work Description	Repetitions	Intensity	Total Time
Aerobic I	5 min. work, 5 min. recovery*	3	60–70%	30 min.
Aerobic II	5 min. work, 5 min. recovery	4	60–70%	40 min.
Aerobic III	4.5 min work, 5 min. recovery	4	70–80%	38 min.
Aerobic IV	4 min. work, 4 min. recovery	5	70–80%	40 min.
Aerobic V	3.5 min. work, 4 min. recovery	5	80–90%	38 min.
Aerobic VI	3 min. work, 3 min. recovery	6	80–90%	36 min.

During recovery period, you should not totally rest, but continue to exercise at an easy intensity (walk slowly, cycle slowly, hang on pool edge and tread slowly, and so on).

Speed

Speed and quickness are critical characteristics of the high-performing athlete in almost all sports. In large part, speed and quickness are things that athletes are born with and can't be taught or trained for. It is not surprising that these attributes are at the top of the list of things looked for by college and professional sport talent scouts. Good coaching can teach the coachable athlete to throw, slide, bat, serve, block, or pass, but no one can be taught to be fast and quick.

There are, however, some things that can be done to improve the efficiency of fast movements, even for the athlete who wasn't born quick, with fast-reacting muscles. Thus, speed training becomes the fifth part of a good conditioning program.

Each of the preceding four conditioning procedures makes a contribution to speed. Muscle strength contributes, particularly in the first few yards of acceleration. Good stretching programs that increase flexibility, fluidity of motion, and efficiency of body movements make small but helpful contributions to speed. Running short distances at speeds greater than are needed in the sport can condition for speed. Most important for the athlete who is not endowed with outstanding speed are so-called specialty exercises that simulate competitive situations encountered in a particular sport. For example, the baseball player practices all-out base running with a quick slide at the end of the circuit. The basketball player repeatedly practices full-court speed dribbling with a lay-up at the end of the court. The soccer player plays one-on-one the full length of the field, setting up a goal shot at the end of the field.

Such drills have a small but somewhat helpful effect on the quickness of muscle response. In addition, they have a very real functional impact as they prompt the athlete to develop good anticipation, a trait that pays off well in games.

Some Basics in Conditioning Programs

The response to training programs and their ultimate effectiveness are largely determined by the attention that is given to certain basic principles operating in all conditioning efforts. These principles include individuality, overload, progression, and specificity.

Individuality

Nowhere is the principle of individuality in conditioning more critical than with very young and new athletes. The response to any conditioning effort will vary greatly among all of us.

Most adults will have, through past experience with muscle work, a pretty good idea of just what kind of training response to expect in comparison to others. However, for young and new athletes, there is no basis of previous experience to tell them whether they will make rapid progress through the progressive steps of the strength or endurance

> **Key Principle**
>
> Potentials for strength, quickness, coordination, intensity of effort, and interest all vary among individuals and all influence the conditioning response.

conditioning chart or whether they are destined to take an extra week at one or more steps before they can move ahead. Nor do they know as yet how far in any conditioning activity their bodies are going to be able to go. These potentials of performance, inherited and genetically determined, have not been tested as yet. It is important for coaches of very young athletes to be understanding and reassuring during these explorations of physical conditioning.

Overload

The key to maximizing response to conditioning is the principle of overload—regularly increasing the intensity of the conditioning effort. The increase may be in the duration of the effort (the amount of work done) or it may be in the rate of work done. The swimmer may induce training overload either by swimming longer distances or by swimming the same distance at a faster speed. Improvement in performance comes only by increasing the demand of the conditioning effort. This is true in all five components of the conditioning program.

Key Principle

All experienced athletes know that the response in performance to overload is not proportional to the degree of overload.

The young field hockey hopeful may run three half-hour sessions each week during preseason and improve her aerobic endurance capacity by 10%. Running every day or six half-hour sessions each week won't improve her aerobic capacity 20%; it will more likely reach only 12 to 15%. The body's ability to respond to overload in general and the individuality of the response to overload must always be kept in mind if frustration and discouragement with the rate of progress are to be kept in proper perspective.

Progression

The change in performance that follows the normal body response to overload is called progression. In a well-disciplined conditioning program, the normal response to overload will be reached in 4 to 6 weeks. Increasing overload in the specific areas demanded of a given sport will, in some individuals, elicit further response. But this latter response comes from progressively greater overloads extended over very prolonged periods of time. A swimmer may work for years to take a few seconds or less off his or her championship time. It may take endless hours of training to add another inch to the elite performance of a high jumper. Rapid responses to overload in early conditioning are followed by slow, tedious responses to the ever-increasing demands of progression.

Specificity

Each specific type of training activity must be recognized as producing a very specific conditioning response. Thus, even in early preseason conditioning, activities will usually be designed to closely simulate the movements and activities involved in the particular sport. Aerobic endurance conditioning will occupy a more prominent part of the conditioning program of the distance runner and basketball player than that of the football candidate or the gymnast. Muscle masses involved in specific sports will receive prime attention in strength conditioning. The closer to the competing season, the more sport-specific the conditioning program will become. The hockey player will look for increasing opportunities to practice on the ice, the basketball player will dribble up and down the court, and the cross-country skier will work more and more on ski trails.

Key Principle
The muscles themselves and the nature of the work they are going to be asked to perform are all very specific to an individual's sport.

Choosing the Right Conditioning Program

The conditioning program outlined here and its five components can meet the conditioning needs of the individual who wishes only to increase feelings of well-being, to support good health, and to enjoy taking part in various recreational activities as they become available. In addition, if pursued with greater intensity over time, this conditioning program will be very adequate to prepare a young athlete for a season of intensely competitive sport. This individual must be involved in the conditioning program for approximately an hour or more each day, 4 or 5 days a week, if he or she is to experience the overload and progression needed for serious sport participation. Such individuals include the high school athlete, the older adolescent involved in community-based youth sport programs, or the collegiate athlete.

What about conditioning for the millions of other youth sport participants: the preadolescent, or elementary, and junior high school-aged athletes? What is an adequate conditioning program for these athletes if they are to truly enjoy sports and be comfortably competitive with their peers?

The answer to these questions is perhaps quite obvious from the information you may have gathered from early chapters of this book:

- First, you should reflect on the appropriate goals of sport participation for this age group of athletes—those under 13 or 14 years of age.

- Second, as was discussed in the chapter on the athlete's body and its behavior in response to athletic performance (Chapter 8), there are limits to just what capabilities the preadolescent body has to respond to a conditioning program.

We believe that the appropriate goals of sport participation prior to the onset of adolescent growth and development are to have fun, encounter a variety of rewarding social experiences, learn some skills and techniques in a low-key emotional environment, and have the benefit of a generous amount of fitness-inducing physical exercise. We do not see specifically getting in shape or developing a high level of physical conditioning as an important goal for the millions of preadolescents in youth sport programs. This is especially true of the very young in their early introduction to sport. One valid reason why intense conditioning with its overload and progression of response is inappropriate at this age is that it simply cannot be looked upon as much fun. It misses the first goal of sport participation for the child.

Good conditioning and warm-up involve skills and techniques just as other parts of sport performance do. When the young athlete begins organized team or club play, he or she can be expected to be introduced to the various skills and techniques of sports. It is hoped that for the preadolescent, the introduction will be by a qualified teacher who uses a positive style of coaching (see Chapter 4).

> **Key Principle**
> More often than not, high school athletes are highly motivated to take part in a good conditioning program.

The interested and motivated young person may begin to train with the no-equipment weight training program outlined in this chapter and should be introduced to good stretching techniques as part of the warm-up procedure for practices and games. Here again, learning the techniques of proper stretching for maintenance of flexibility for future, more serious sport participation is the goal. The approach should be relaxed, with little concern if a few repetitions are missed in the workout.

There is no doubt that good preseason, in-season, and off-season conditioning programs are of tremendous help to the committed high school athlete, the young person who, among other reasons, is into the athletic program to see just what kind of a new body he or she can develop. Some want to do it alone and on their own, whereas others truly enjoy various group conditioning activities. Weight training classes, clubs, and conditioning groups are increasingly popular. Many coaches plan specific off-season team conditioning programs for their athletes. If well supervised and directed toward proper goals, conditioning activities should be encouraged among high school youths. For many it may be the beginning of a serious commitment to lifelong fitness that prepares them for enjoyable participation in a variety of active recreational-sport activities. Attending to the five components of a conditioning program can provide an effective foundation for conditioning for high school sports as well as for fitness in later life.

Conditioning programs are appropriate only where they are compatible with proper sport goals for the age of the athlete. An age group of particular concern is the early adolescent, the individual just beginning his or her rapid gain in height and very anxious about their new and changing physique. These young people, particularly the males, often direct great effort to very intense conditioning. Intense weight training may be undertaken to increase muscle size or strength, but early adolescents may have little potential yet, except for a very significant increase in the risk of injury if the weight program is unsupervised and overdone. We find in this group many distance runners who run to an extreme, which, when excessive, will lead to weight loss, growth arrest, and weakness. Such excessive endurance training will make little if any contribution to physical development and athletic potential.

Early adolescents need to be informed of their developmental status. This may be best done by an understanding physician, who may give some insight as to when body changes will be such that bodies can be expected to respond to an intense conditioning program. Most vulnerable in such abuses of training are late maturers. Intense conditioning activities do not hasten the maturation process, unfortunately, and conditioning excesses by these young people should be tempered for a few years. Currently, endocrine specialists are able to provide help to some very late maturing males who become seriously distressed about their maturation and development during their junior high school and high school years. In carefully selected individuals, it is possible to hasten maturation with well-controlled endocrine therapy.

Key Principle

As increasing millions of Americans begin to assume greater responsibility for their own health and fitness, conditioning programs and new fitness techniques become more important and popular.

The very young preadolescent will profit from being introduced to proper techniques of conditioning and warm-up. The later adolescent and the high school athlete cannot fully enjoy their sport or be competitive without good conditioning programs. At this important time, as young people develop to their adult years, good physical conditioning techniques and practices can have lifelong benefits.

Drugs and the Young Athlete

As we have become painfully aware in recent years, the use of performance enhancing drugs and supplements has invaded the world of sports as never before. The scary fact is that the use of body-enhancing substances has begun to appear even at the youth sport level, and they are readily available to the young athlete who has the money and poor judgment to purchase them. These chemical agents are not only outlawed in sports, but many of them are known to have devastating long-term effects on the body. Two drugs commonly found in the locker room are amphetamines ("speed") and anabolic steroids (synthetic derivatives of the natural male hormone testosterone).

Amphetamines, although more common on the sport scene a few years ago than today, are still around. They are powerful nervous-system stimulants. They give the athlete an exaggerated sense of performance, reduce powers of perception, alter fine coordination, and increase the risk of injury. The altered, hyped-up, and inappropriate agitation of the amphetamine user usually make the speed freak obvious in the pregame locker room. Any user will need some information and counseling. Further steps may be required if the amphetamines are being provided by a misguided parent.

Key Principle
The young person freaked out on amphetamines is not going to be very competitive on any sport team.

Anabolic steroids are particularly attractive to young men who are weightlifters, body builders, football players, shot-putters, discus throwers, and swimmers. The young man trying to increase body weight and muscle mass with a program of increased food intake and weight training will sooner or later encounter some "gym rat" who has hormone capsules or injections to peddle. Dianabol is one of the common trade names for steroids.

Do anabolic steroids increase muscle size and strength? When normal healthy men take steroids without training, there is no effect on muscle size or strength. However, most studies show that anabolic steroids in high doses combined with heavy resistance training will result in an increase in body weight and muscle size. And, in most research subjects, high doses of steroids combined with training will result in increases in strength. Whether this increase in strength results in improved athletic performance is a debatable issue.

What level of dosage is required? Anabolic steroids are sometimes used medically to treat patients with certain blood disorders (e.g., anemia), severe burns, endocrine gland abnormalities, and malnutrition. They are also used to counter the negative effects of radiation and chemotherapy for cancer patients. Normal therapeutic doses range from 30 to 60 milligrams per day. In comparison, body builders usually take 200 milligrams of Dianabol per day—a dangerously high amount.

Key Principle
Anabolic steroids will, in the long run, take their harmful toll.

What are the hazards/dangers associated with steroid use? Studies have uncovered a wide variety of ill effects, including the following:

- Heart disease. This is caused by a dramatic rise in the level of low-density (bad) lipoprotein cholesterol and a drop in protective high-density lipoprotein cholesterol.

- Sexual and reproductive disorders. When men take steroids, their own testosterone production is inhibited, which can result in atrophy of the testicles, loss of libido (sex drive), impotence, and enlargement of the breasts. In women, steroids can cause menstrual irregularities and infertility. The drugs can also have pronounced masculinizing effects, such as facial hair, diminished breast size, permanently deepened voice and thinning of the hair. Acne may develop or worsen in both sexes.

- Immune deficiencies. Steroids cause a significant suppression of the white blood cells that produce antibodies, as well as those that fight off viruses and cancer.

- Liver disorders. Steroid users risk serious liver damage, including jaundice, tumors, and gallstones.

- Stunted growth. In young people who have not yet completed growth, steroids can prematurely close the growth plates in their long bones and permanently stunt their growth.

- Psychological disturbances. Steroid use by athletes has been linked to increased fighting and other aggressive behavior (e.g., the so-called roid rage). Former wives of some football players who have used steroids said their husbands became superaggressive and sexually violent. Other psychological disturbances include unhealthy mood swings—psychotic episodes and extreme euphoria. Moreover, severe depression can occur when use of steroids is discontinued.

Key Principle

Lyle Alzado, a star professional football player, campaigned against the use of anabolic steroids before his death from cancer, which was attributed to steroid effects.

The latest fad is the use of creatine supplements, which increase the normal level of a natural body substance (testosterone) that energizes muscles. Creatine supplements allow the muscles to work longer and harder, and they have been shown to result in an increase in endurance and recovery from fatigue, and the ability to train harder. However, the long-term effects of creatine supplements are unknown. Nonetheless, there is enough concern that several professional football teams have forbidden their athletes to use creatine. As a coach, you should be equally concerned.

It is important to counsel youngsters against the chemical "shortcuts" to strength and performance enhancement. These substances are out there and are used by even some preadolescent athletes. The glamor of athletic stardom is so great for many young people that they are vulnerable to the use of substances that may have negative effects on their future health and well-being. The strength of temptation was shown in one study in which high school athletes were asked if they would be willing to take a drug that would reduce their life span by 10 years but would also result in their ability to have a career in professional sports. The vast majority of the athletes said that they would take the drug. In today's world, the watchword is BEWARE.

Sport Injuries

Serious injuries are not common in sports. This is particularly true for athletes less than 14 years of age. Their small size and limited strength combine with safety rules and adult supervision to help minimize the risk of significant injury. Sport injuries become more common in high school, where the intensity of competition increases along with the size and strength of the participants.

Fortunately, regardless of age, most athletes will not suffer serious sport injuries, and when properly managed, injuries will limit training and competition for no more than a few days. Because responsibility for the recognition and management of sport-related injuries often falls on coaches, there is some essential information that you should have about their nature and treatment.

Key Principle

Older and stronger athletes are more capable of causing injury to themselves and to their opponents.

What Is a Sport Injury?

There are certain symptoms of sport injuries that should be recognized as such by coaches and athletes alike. These include:

- Bleeding.
- Mental confusion or loss of consciousness.
- Numbness or tingling of an extremity.

- A recognizable deformity of any body part.

- Instability of any joint, such as a knee that "wobbles."

- The sound of tearing or ripping at the time of injury.

- Localized swelling or pain.

- Absence of a full range of motion of any joint.

An athlete with any of these symptoms should not return to play or practice until a very specific diagnosis of the nature of the injury has been made and the symptoms of injury have completely disappeared. Any of these injuries can easily be made worse by continued participation. Unable to move normally and protect themselves when injured, athletes with any of these symptoms are at high risk for a new injury.

> 🔑 *Key Principle*
> The most common sport-related injuries are the so-called overuse injuries, the too-much, too-soon, too-fast injuries

Overuse injuries result from the excessive or improper use of some body part, most often tendons and muscles. Overuse injuries are often identified with certain sports or types of activities. There is the jogger's heel, the jumper's knee, the tennis elbow, the swimmer's shoulder, the Little League elbow, and so on. All are the result of overuse of a specified muscle or tendon unit in training for a certain sport.

In collision sports, such as football, wrestling, ice hockey, and lacrosse, the most common injuries are bumps, bruises, and lacerations. In both collision and running sports, muscles, tendons, and ligaments can be stretched or torn in strains and sprains, although most of these possible injuries tend to be minor ones.

The coach of an injured athlete must assume primary responsibility for the proper management of a sport injury, initiating and following a safe and effective management plan that will assure the athlete's return to participation as quickly and as safely as possible. Prompt treatment and effective follow-through on a sound treatment plan are most important. Postponing care or failing to follow the prescribed treatment plan will prolong discomfort, hamper performance, and greatly increase the risk of reinjury.

Athletes should be instructed to inform you or the athletic trainer about any injury immediately, so that they can be promptly treated and returned to the game or practice as soon as possible. Attempting to "tough it out" and play through pain can harm both the athlete and the team. It is better to stay out of practice for two or three days while an injury is being properly treated and return to action only when fully recovered.

Things NOT to Do if Injured in Sport

Here are some important *don'ts* to emphasize to athletes:

- *Don't* try to hide an injury. Report the injury to the coach or trainer.
- *Don't* apply treatment other than simple first aid until a specific diagnosis has been made by the trainer or a doctor.
- *Don't* apply heat to an injury without orders from the doctor. A common but mistaken belief is that heat helps a new injury. By increasing swelling, it can actually make things worse rather than better.
- *Don't* use an injured part if it hurts. More pain means more injury.
- *Don't* take any drugs unless they are prescribed by a physician.
- *Don't* tape or splint an injured part without specific instructions from a doctor.
- *Don't* go back to practice or competition until you have a full range of motion, full strength (both sides are equally strong), and full function of the injured part.

These *don'ts* should be modified only under the direct orders of a physician or a certified athletic trainer (not a volunteer or student trainer). The quickest and safest way to get back into active participation is to limit activity as long as there is any pain or swelling, then to follow rigidly a prescribed rehabilitation program, which will include a schedule of specifically planned exercises. In specialized sports medicine clinics, the patient problem most frequently seen is the athlete with an inadequately rehabilitated sport injury who returned to his or her sport and was reinjured. In a large study of high school football injuries, 50% of those injured were reinjured when they returned to participation—a sad commentary on injury management.

Things to Do When Injured

The athlete's first responsibility when injured is to get out of the game or practice. Continued participation may make the injury worse and may place the athlete at increased risk to another injury. A healthy substitute is better for the team than an injured all-star.

When leaving the field or court, the athlete should avoid using the injured part. The player should support an injured arm or wrist (with a sling if possible) and get support so he or she won't walk on an injured leg or ankle.

> *Key Principle*
> Never apply heat to a sports injury unless it is ordered by a physician.

Promptly apply the only first-aid treatment that is safe for treatment of a sports injury without professional advice—**ICE** (**I** for ice, **C** for compression, and **E** for elevation). The **ICE** treatment is easily available and easily applied on the sidelines at games and practices. All that is needed are plastic bags (from the supermarket produce counter), crushed ice, and a picnic cooler, which holds the bags of crushed ice and some wet 4-inch elastic bandages.

To apply the **ICE** treatment, remove any part of the uniform that surrounds the injured area and elevate the arm or leg above the level of the heart. Apply one layer of the cold, wet elastic bandage on the skin directly over the injury, put the plastic bag of ice on the bandage, and firmly wrap the remainder of the bandage around the bag of ice. Keep the ice and the compression wrap on the elevated, immobilized injury for 25 to 30 minutes. As long as there is pain and/or swelling, keep the injury elevated. Avoid standing or walking on a painful leg or ankle before or after the ice application. **ICE** treatment for 25 to 30 minutes may be applied four or more times a day for a few days following an injury. If pain or swelling persists, see a physician.

When a girl sprains her ankle in a basketball game and its supporting ligaments are stretched and torn, or when a wide receiver strains and ruptures the fibers of a hamstring muscle, a sequence of events occurs that is common to all such sport injuries. Blood vessels are damaged and some will break, allowing blood and fluid to accumulate in the injured area. This causes increased pressure, swelling, and pain, and the pressure and swelling cause further damage and injury to the surrounding tissues.

This reaction of the body to injury has a protective function as well. The pain of the initial injury causes the muscles of the injured area to go into further painful spasms. This limits movement and discourages the use of the injured area, thereby preventing further injury.

> *Key Principle*
>
> When properly applied, **ICE** treatments can do no harm to any type of injury.

The **ICE** treatment helps in three important ways:

- First, applying ice chills the bruised or injured area, causing blood vessels to contract and reducing circulation to the injured area—quite the opposite of what heat applications might do.

- Second, applying pressure with the elastic bandage inhibits the accumulation of blood and fluids in the area, thereby minimizing painful and damaging swelling.

- Finally, elevating the injury decreases fluid accumulation in the injured area, puts the area at rest, and helps reduce painful muscle spasms.

When applied promptly and repeatedly, **ICE** treatments significantly reduce the discomfort and period of limited activity resulting from an injury. Almost anything else—including heat applications—can cause harm in some instances.

Preventing Sport Injuries

Everyone involved in youth sports—coaches, athletes, administrators, and parents—should constantly seek practical ways to minimize the risk of sport injury. Here are some things you can do to reduce the risk of injury:

- Assure that competition is between persons with similar levels of proficiency, maturity, size, and strength. This is particularly important in the collision sports, where the risk of injury is greatest. The less-skilled and smaller players get more than their share of injuries in such sports.

• Be sure that athletes are at appropriate levels of conditioning before they turn out for practice or attempt vigorous competition. A good idea is to talk to athletes 2 or 3 months prior to the first workouts, and give them suggestions for a preseason conditioning program. The unconditioned athlete gets injured early in the season, sometimes seriously. Basic conditioning guidelines are presented in Chapter 9.

• Be certain that protective equipment is available and used. Protective equipment has been developed and provided for good reasons. Be sure it fits, that it doesn't need repair, and that it is used properly.

• Most sports are played on the feet. Be certain that shoes and socks fit and that socks are clean and without holes. Many troublesome foot problems can be prevented.

• Don't wear jewelry in active sports. Neck jewelry can be dangerous; rings can produce serious finger injury by getting caught in basket nets, uniforms, and so on.

• Practice good hygiene. Skin infections are common among athletes and can keep an athlete out of training for a week or more of expensive treatment. They can also spread to other team members. Showering with an antibacterial soap daily is a good practice to reduce the risk of skin infections. Keep all uniforms laundered and clean.

• Fingernails should always be trimmed shorter than the tip of the finger to prevent painful scratches and potentially serious eye injuries. This is especially important in basketball.

• Never play with a fever. Otherwise mild, common viral infections can become serious illness following a hard workout or game. Stay home; the risk of passing an infection on to other team members should always be avoided. A good rule is that with fever over 100 degrees, stay home and get well.

- Whether at a school or community venue, take a minute to be sure that anything a player may run into or get injured from is well away from the playing area. Bicycles, benches, lawn mowers, sprinklers, scorers' tables, and other obstacles can all cause serious injuries.

Be Prepared for an Emergency

Most injuries occurring in sports are minor, but on very rare occasions, serious, life-threatening injuries occur. These emergencies usually have to be managed on the scene before any medical help is available. We therefore recommend that coaches do one thing before getting involved any further in sports: Get certified in CPR (cardiopulmonary resuscitation). CPR training is available through the American Red Cross, local fire departments, schools, or Boy/Girl Scout programs.

> *Key Principle*
> Training in CPR teaches the basic life-saving techniques that can keep a seriously injured athlete alive until emergency medical aid arrives.

An accident or injury to an athlete that results in any of the following symptoms presents a serious emergency that demands the skills of CPR training and prompt medical assistance:

- Not breathing.
- Unconscious.
- Bleeding
- In shock—particularly during hot weather.

Injured athletes in these conditions can die before medical assistance arrives on the scene if someone isn't prepared to initiate thoughtful action. Before your next game or practice, take 10 seconds and think through exactly how you would get emergency help if one of those very rare but life-threatening injuries should occur. You must know:

- Where is there a telephone?
- Whom do you call for help? (dial 911)
- What is the location of the field or gym?

- Will the emergency vehicle be able to get on the field? If there is a locked gate, who has the key?

If you don't know these things, you may be helpless when the crisis occurs. Someone's son or daughter or teammate could die because no one was prepared for the unexpected.

Earlier we listed some important *don'ts* for sport injuries in general. The following recommendations are even more critical because of the life-threatening nature of some serious injuries:

- *Don't* move an unconscious athlete any more than needed for CPR.

- *Don't* move any athlete who can't move all four extremities freely.

- *Don't* remove the helmet from any unconscious athlete. You may seriously compound a possible injury to the spine.

- *Don't* use ammonia capsules to attempt to revive an athlete who may be unconscious or "dinged." They can complicate a neck or spine injury and may cause face and eye burns.

Much of the fun and satisfaction of sport participation comes from extending oneself to maximum effort. Such stresses may on occasion result in injury. Although most injuries are not serious, they do interfere temporarily with one's ability to compete and can result in more serious injuries if not cared for properly. Know how to manage the more common, less severe injuries that will be sustained by young athletes. Don't let them become more severe than need be or lead to a needlessly prolonged period of disability.

When Injury Prevents Participation

Should an athlete be allowed to play when injured or ill? As a general rule, it is never appropriate to play an injured or ill youngster.

How do you know when an injury or illness is sufficiently severe to remove a youngster from a game, or to withhold an athlete from a practice or game? The decision should be based on a strong dose of common sense. For example, a sprained ankle or a pulled hamstring

> **Key Principle**
>
> Never encourage an athlete to play with pain, for there is a strong possibility of making the injury more serious.

muscle is stronger grounds for nonparticipation than a bruised arm because of the greater risk of worsening the injury. And if you are uncertain about it, be sure to consult with a sports medicine specialist.

What can be done when a sport injury prevents participation? A young athlete may be temporarily eliminated from a sport program because of an injury. This may be less painful to the athlete's self-esteem than being cut, but can in many ways be just as frustrating. One of the disappointments of being injured is that the youngster no longer feels a full part of the team.

You can counteract this by making sure the injured athlete is included in team practices and games in some way. For example, an injured softball player can coach the bases and keep the scorebook.

Another constructive activity for the injured athlete is mental rehearsal. You can recommend that the athlete who cannot participate actively during practice do so by using imagery, and injured athletes should be encouraged to mentally practice their skills. Many injured athletes have reported that they maintained their skill level or even performed at a higher level when they returned because of the use of mental rehearsal.

Can You Be Sued?

It is no secret that we live in an age where people feel free to seek legal redress for real or imagined wrongs. Anyone who occupies a position that can affect the welfare of children, including the youth coach, has a rightful (and legal) responsibility to provide a safe experience. A coach who fails to carry out this responsibility (either by acting irresponsibly or by failing to act responsibly) can be sued and found guilty of negligence.

Technically, a judgment of negligence requires that (a) you have a legal duty, (b) you failed to fulfill that legal duty, and (c) someone sustained injury as a result of your failure to fulfill the duty. Under these conditions, you can be found guilty and be subject to substantial financial penalties.

During the past 25 years, an increasing number of lawsuits have been filed against youth sport coaches, and the court decisions in these cases have established the legal responsibilities of coaches. Awareness of these responsibilities can help you to carry them out in a manner that enhances the welfare of young athletes as well as your ability to defend yourself against litigation.

1. *Provide a safe physical environment.* Inspect the facility, making sure there are no hazards, such as holes, broken glass, exposed sprinkler heads, or sharp corners. If there are hazards that you cannot remedy, warn your athletes about them and steer activity away from them as much as possible.

2. *Provide proper and safe equipment.* Baseball bats with loose hand grips or masks with cracked bars, or loose bolts in diving boards or gymnastics equipment are accidents waiting to happen. Many a suit has been filed when unsafe equipment caused an injury. Inspect equipment regularly and teach your athletes how to inspect their equipment and use it correctly. A football helmet that is used to butt, ram, or spear an opponent with its crown can cause severe spinal injuries, and a failure to warn an athlete about misuse of the helmet can have severe consequences for the coach as well as the athlete.

3. *Plan the activity properly.* Plan your practices and suit them to the current physical conditioning and skill levels of your athletes, allowing for individual differences. Do not practice advanced skills until your athletes are ready for them, for they may be dangerous for unprepared youngsters. Likewise, adapt conditioning to the current physical conditioning of your team. Asking children to run a mile the first day of practice is asking for trouble.

4. *Provide safe and proper instruction.* Learn how to teach the skills of your sport safely through reading or coaching clinics. Recent judgments against coaches have taught us that many commonly seen practices, such as sliding head-first in baseball, are unsafe and should never be taught or even permitted by coaches.

5. *Provide close supervision.* You are formally responsible for all activities that occur during a practice session, so be aware of what is going on. If you have to leave the area, make sure that an assistant is present.

6. *Warn athletes and parents of inherent risks.* Every sport has risks associated with it, and many a suit has been based on the claim, "I was never warned that this could happen." Youth sport programs have tried to protect themselves by including discussions of foreseeable risks in parent orientation meetings and on parental consent forms. Likewise, athletes should be warned of such risks and told what to do if they occur (for example, if a gymnast falls and strikes her head). The goal here is not to frighten parents and athletes unduly, but rather, to give them a reasonable basis for informed consent to participate in the program.

7. *Match your athletes on physical and skill attributes.* The responsibility here is to avoid placing youngsters at risk by matching them against others who are much larger, stronger, or physically skilled. As mentioned above, this is particularly important in collision sports like football and wrestling. One-on-one contact drills between a 100 pound football player and a 200 pound youngster reflects poor judgment on the coach's part and can be the basis for a negligence judgment.

8. *Evaluate athletes for injury, illness, or incapacity.* Another situation that can place an athlete at significant physical risk is health problems or a previous injury. Many programs require a preparticipation physical exam to ensure that athletes do not have a health problem or unhealed injury that could be dangerous. This responsibility also pertains to judgments of when an injured athlete can resume participation. One general guideline is that an athlete who has been knocked unconscious during a contest should not be returned to action, for it is possible that undetectable physical damage has occurred.

9. *Provide adequate medical assistance.* In the event of a serious injury, the coach is responsible for securing appropriate medical assistance. Again, know where the nearest phone is and the number to call. Never move a severely injured athlete. Every coach should take a general first-aid course and learn CPR.

10. *Keep adequate records.* In the event of litigation, it will be essential to have written records to demonstrate that you carried out your responsibilities. Practice plans and a record of exactly what was done following an injury, who was notified, etc. can be critically important.

11. Obtain liability insurance. As lawsuits have multiplied, the necessity of having adequate liability insurance (at least $1 million worth) has become increasingly evident. Find out what kinds of coverage are provided by your sport program, which should have a policy. If its coverage is inadequate, a low-cost addition to your homeowner's insurance may provide the protection you need.

Obviously, we have merely scratched the surface of sport law in this summary of coaches' legal responsibilities. Several useful sources for additional information are provided in the reference section at the end of the book.

Part 5

Coaching Challenges and How to Deal with Them

Approaches to Dealing with "Problem Athletes"

No matter how much you think in terms of the team, in reality that team is made up of unique individuals. Many outstanding coaches have emphasized the importance of being able to relate to athletes as individuals, of gaining insight into what makes each athlete "tick," and of using that knowledge to help the athlete get the most out of himself or herself.

The name of this game is flexibility. Being flexible does not mean having different rules for different athletes, any more than fairness means treating everyone exactly alike. Team rules must hold for everyone, or discipline and respect break down quickly. On the other hand, knowledge of and respect for the makeup of each individual can be a key to successful coaching.

Athletes come in all shapes, sizes, and personality types. Some are a joy to coach, while others create problems for themselves and other people. Most coaches have had one or more athletes whom they have found difficult to handle. Others have known athletes whose psychological makeup limited their capacity to enjoy their sport experience or to perform up to their potential.

Left unattended, conduct problems or emotional difficulties can affect the success and enjoyment of coach and athletes alike. This in itself would be sufficient justification

> **Key Principle**
>
> Sports can be a growth experience for problem athletes, but dealing with these athletes requires additional knowledge, understanding, and patience on the part of coaches.

for trying to do something constructive about them. But another and equally important reason for discussing these problems is that the experiences a young athlete has in sports can help undo previous life experiences that have led to the problems. A sensitive and informed coach can promote a sport experience that helps the athlete to learn new attitudes and problem solving skills that improve personal adjustment. We believe firmly that the demands of the sport environment, together with the efforts of a sensitive and caring coach, can help to "build character" in a manner that few other settings can.

Although the job description of youth coach does not include the term "amateur psychologist," most coaches come to realize sooner or later that they are, in part, exactly that. And the most effective coaches are darn good amateur psychologists in the sense that they know how to influence athletes in ways that help them grow as people, not just as skilled performers.

"Problem" athletes fall into a number of different groups. We will describe some of the more common types, together with the kinds of life experiences that are likely to have produced the problems. Then we will describe methods that have proven successful in dealing with and, hopefully, helping such athletes.

The Uncoachable Child

One of the most frustrating problems to deal with is the athlete who resists coaching. Such athletes often will not listen to instructions or follow them, or they insist on doing things *their* way. Sometimes their resistance is expressed as open defiance and insistence that they know better than you how things should be done. In other cases their resistance is never openly expressed but comes out indirectly. They may nod as if they're listening to you, then go and do as they please. This kind of indirect resistance can be even harder to deal with than the direct kind.

> ⚷ *Key Principle*
> Resistance may be expressed as open defiance or more subtly as doing as one pleases.

"Uncoachable" or resistant athletes are frequently acting out unresolved problems in dealing with earlier authority figures. They usually have had negative experiences with people in power positions (especially father figures) who have forced them to do things against their will. Or, especially in cases involving divorce, they may view themselves as having been deserted or betrayed by the authority figure. They now carry their scars and residue of anger into other relationships with authority figures and resist them. In other cases, resistance is a part of the normal adolescent pattern of testing limits and challenging authority as a part of establishing independence. This "normal" resistance can usually be overcome by setting clear and reasonable guidelines and showing that you are going to insist upon compliance.

The natural tendency is simply to confront resistant athletes and tell them to "shape up, or else." Sometimes this solves the problem but it is best to do this only as a last resort, especially if you want to help the athlete resolve the underlying problem. When you react in this manner you may be doing exactly what past authority figures did to create the problem. Moreover, the athlete may agree to shape up, only to begin resisting you in new indirect ways.

In the long run, what will help the resistant athlete most is a relationship with an authority figure who is firm, yet caring and trustworthy. This may take some time if the underlying problem is a severe one.

> *Key Principle*
>
> The resistant athlete is frequently acting out unresolved problems with authority figures. He or she may need exposure to a firm but caring coaching style.

In the beginning, you may find it helpful to say something like "I have a hunch you've had some problems with people in authority in the past, and that these problems are coming out in this situation. I hope you'll find me to be a different person than they, but that will take time. In the meantime I expect you to do what you're supposed to just like everyone else, and the amount of playing time you get will depend on that. If you have a question about why we're doing something my way, feel free to ask me about it, but do so at a time and place that doesn't interfere with what we're about."

Like any other set of behaviors, "coachability" can be strengthened through reinforcement. Rather than taking the chance of increasing resistance by using punishment to try to force compliance, try using the positive approach to get the desired behaviors. Set clear expectations and, rather than taking compliance for granted, recognize and reinforce it when it occurs: "Way to go. You did exactly what we're trying to get across. That's the way to listen and execute!" This kind of approach makes you a different kind of authority figure than the ones the athlete may still be struggling against, and it helps build a positive rather than an adversarial relationship.

The Spoiled Brat

Another coach's "delight," these athletes are selfish and wrapped up in themselves. They care little about anything except what *they* can get from participating. They usually come across as very sincere and nice, but this is a phony front that they use to con other people into giving them what they want. They will also pit people against one another to achieve their selfish goals. Such athletes believe that team rules and expectations are for others, not for "special" people like themselves. Before long they are violating rules, but they have a million excuses for doing so. Over time it becomes clear that they are unwilling to put the team ahead of themselves and do not want to cooperate unless they get some personal glory out of it.

These athletes typically have one of two different life history patterns. Some of them have been babied and pampered all their lives. They have never had limits placed on their behavior—they could do no wrong. As a result, they've grown up in an unrealistic world in which they were the centerpiece. They have no reason to believe that their athletic experience should be any different.

Other egocentric athletes have had quite the opposite life experiences. They have grown up in families where no one cared about them. They have had to learn to get what they want for themselves. The name of the game is "looking out for Number One," and they have become quite adept at manipulating others in order to achieve their ends.

Regardless of which pattern of life experiences is responsible, these athletes have to be told in no uncertain terms that there are definable limits and punishments for breaking the rules. The spoiled brat needs to learn

> **Key Principle**
>
> "No special deals. There's no way you can have a team concept if one player knows that another player is getting a little bit more."
>
> Don James, former University of Washington football coach

that no individual is more important than the team and that team goals take priority over individual goals. There are no special favors. Those who fit the first pattern described above can be told in a straightforward manner that the sport situation may be different from others they've been in. Those of the second pattern, who tend to see life as "dog eat dog," may need to be dealt with more sternly. The message must be that the only way they are going to get what they want out of the sport experience is to take others' needs into account as well as their own.

The sport experience can be one in which self-centered athletes learn that life involves give as well as take, and that considerable satisfaction can come from being a part of something larger than themselves. For the formerly deprived athlete, it can be a situation where mutual concern and caring are experienced for the first time.

The Low Self-Esteem Child

These athletes have an inferiority complex. Their poor self-image may be limited to one or a few areas of their lives, or they may feel generally inferior to others. In sports, this comes across as a lack of confidence in their abilities, a reluctance to try to get better, or a lack of assertiveness. When they experience setbacks they tend to see them as more evidence that they are inadequate. When they do well, on the other hand, they do not take credit for it. They attribute success to outside factors, such as luck or poor performance by their opponent. This pattern of taking personal credit for failures but not for successes helps to perpetuate their low opinion of themselves.

Such athletes have usually not enjoyed much success in the past, and often they have been made fun of or had their inadequacies pointed out to them. They compare themselves unfavorably with others who are more successful, and they often set standards that are unrealistic or impossible to meet. They get into a way of thinking that "If I'm not the best, I'm the worst." Because they feel inferior, they act inferior, or they try to get attention in ways that get them into more problems.

This is one type of problem that can really be helped by the kind of philosophy of success that we have discussed throughout the book. Low self-esteem people get that way partly because they focus almost

Key Principle

Feelings of inferiority help breed inferior performance as a self-fulfilling prophesy. Such athletes need a supportive environment, a focus on doing one's best, and constant reinforcement of their efforts to improve.

entirely on external outcomes over which they may have little control. They need to learn that success comes from *doing your best* rather than *being the best*. The focus with such athletes needs to be on individual goal setting and improvement that they can take personal pride in, and on the communication of caring and the conviction that they are worthwhile people. The goal-setting and performance feedback approaches described in Chapter 5 can be very helpful for such athletes, for they can clearly see the results of their efforts and can't write them off as being due to chance or luck. If you can help them learn to take pride in their efforts and their willingness to put themselves on the line, the sport experience can be a turning point for them. With time their efforts will result in successes that increase their self-confidence.

The kind of team climate that you help create can be very important for low self-concept athletes. Using the positive approach yourself, and emphasizing to your athletes that you expect them to support and encourage their teammates, can promote a positive interpersonal environment that gives plenty of social support to everyone, from star to bench warmer. In such an environment the athlete who lacks confidence can get the support needed to begin to revise an inferior self-concept. Remember to use your "reinforcement power" to strengthen the desired support behaviors when they occur initially. After a while they tend to occur on their own because they create positive outcomes for everyone involved.

The Hyperanxious Child

These athletes become tense and "psyched out" in competition. They tend to be very inconsistent in their performance level and have a tendency to perform poorly in pressure situations. Many of them display great talent in practice situations, but "choke" and fall apart in contests. They are also prone to use injuries as a way of avoiding the challenges of competition.

You will recognize this pattern as indicative of the high fear of failure athlete discussed in Chapter 6. As we indicated there, the most common cause of high anxiety is a previous history of punishment or criticism for failure outcomes and a failure to reinforce effort. As a result they feel threatened by achievement situations.

At the core of this problem are feelings of lack of control of outcomes and emotional responses. Hyperanxious athletes feel that they cannot control their anxiety, nor can they control the possibility of failing. The key is to give them feelings of greater control over both. The first step is to get them to focus on effort, over which they have complete control, rather than outcome, over which they have limited control. This relates to the philosophy of winning that we discussed in Chapter 2. These athletes need to know that they will be supported whether they win or lose, if they give all they have. In the words of coach Joe Paterno: "You can't ever be afraid to lose. You prepare as best you can, then you plunge in and let it all hang out." Getting this idea across to athletes helps reduce anxiety about failure. They need to learn to separate self-worth from performance so they can enjoy the demands of competition.

Another approach to helping overanxious athletes gain control is to teach the emotional control skills described in Chapter 6. Athletes who feel a lack of control over their anxiety can gain a massive dose of self-confidence when they learn relaxation skills. Knowing that one can control nervousness and tension gives hyperanxious athletes new feelings of control and a better chance of performing up to their capabilities. Ability to control body and mind is the stuff of which mental toughness is made.

The Withdrawn Child

These athletes seem to avoid getting close to others, and it is hard to involve them in the team. They may actively avoid being involved in activities with the rest of the team. More than simple shyness seems to be involved; there is a sense that they are afraid of close relationships with others. Others sometimes react to them with hostility because they misinterpret their standoffishness as resulting from feelings of superiority and feel rejected.

This pattern of avoidance of closeness often results from having been deeply hurt in close relationships with people who were important to them. They may have been let down, rejected, or painfully exploited in the past. This resulted in a fear of getting close to others and risking the vulnerability that closeness creates. As much as they may wish they could get close, they find it safer to maintain a barrier against being hurt again.

This is not the kind of problem that goes away immediately. Simply saying "You can trust me" is not going to be enough. You will need to prove yourself again and again by passing "trust tests." Be very straightforward and completely honest. Don't try to say things to build up the athlete unless you can document them. Be supportive and encourage the athlete to interact with others, but do not force him or her to do so. The sport environment can be one in which this athlete can gradually test the waters of relationships and experience the comraderie that is such an important part of athletics.

> **Key Principle**
>
> The withdrawn athlete has often been hurt in previous relationships and fears getting close to others. Demonstrating that you care and establishing trust are critical.

Problems with athletes can take many forms and we have touched upon only a few of the more common varieties. Dealing with such athletes can be a demanding task that tries the patience of a saint. There may be problems that are so disruptive that you have no choice but to exclude the athlete for the good of the program, or instances in which severe personality problems indicate the need for professional attention. You are certainly not expected to function as a professional psychotherapist, nor should you try to in the case of severe personal problems. But, you may be able to create an athletic experience that can have a significant positive impact on athletes who come to you with a previous life history that has resulted in personal problems. What more could any youngster hope to derive from athletics?

Relating Effectively to Youth Sport Parents

Two important sets of adults combine with the child to form the athletic triangle. They are, of course, coaches and parents. The relationships that exist among the points of the athletic triangle go a long way toward determining the quality of the experience that the child has in sports. Therefore your role in dealing with parents can be very important to the success of your program.

Through their cooperative efforts, many parents productively contribute to youth sport programs. Unfortunately the negative impact that some parents have is all too obvious. Out of ignorance they can undermine the basic goals of youth sports and rob youngsters of benefits they could derive from participation. We hope that as a coach you will be able to channel parents' genuine concerns and good intentions in a way that supports what you are trying to accomplish. This chapter provides information to assist you in working effectively with parents, thereby increasing the chances of a desirable sport outcome for all concerned.

Roles and Responsibilities of Parents

When a child enters a sport program, the mother and father automatically take on some obligations. Some parents do not realize this at first and are surprised to find what is expected of them. Others never realize their responsibilities and therefore miss opportunities to help their children grow through sports, or actually do things that interfere with their children's development.

Key Principle

Parents should realize that children not only have a right to participate in sports but also to choose *not* to participate.

To begin, parents must realize that children have a right to participate in sports. This includes the right to choose *not* to participate. Although parents might choose to encourage participation, children should not be pressured, intimidated, or bribed into playing. If children feel forced, their chances of receiving the benefits of sports are decreased. Even more profound and long-lasting are the effects that feeling forced can have on parent-child relationships. Just how profound is shown in this statement made by a 40-year-old man: "If it hadn't been for sports, I wouldn't have grown up hating my father."

In fulfilling their responsibility, parents should counsel their children, giving consideration to the sport selected and the level of competition at which the children want to play. And, of course, parents should respect their children's decisions.

Sometimes the best decision is not to participate. Participation in sports, although desirable, is not necessarily for everyone. For those

Key Principle

"Parents should be observers and supporters of their athletically inclined children, but never pushers."

Wayne Gretzky, former professional hockey player

children who wish to direct their energies in other ways, the best program may be no program. Many parents become unnecessarily alarmed if their child does not show an interest in sports—particularly if the parents themselves had positive sport experiences. They think that a child who would rather do other things must somehow be abnormal. But forcing a child into sports against his or her will can be a big mistake. Sometimes the wisest decision is to encourage the child to move into other activities that may be more suited to his or her interests and abilities, at least until an interest in sports develops.

Parents can enjoy their children's participation more if they acquire an understanding and appreciation of the sport. This includes knowledge of basic rules, skills, and strategies. As a coach, you can serve as a valuable resource by answering parents' questions and by referring parents to a community/school library or a bookstore for educational materials. In addition, you might devote part of an early season practice to a lecture/demonstration of the fundamentals of the sport. Parents having little background in the sport should be encouraged to attend this session.

Some parents unknowingly become a source of stress to young athletes. All parents identify with their children to some extent and thus want them to do well. Unfortunately, in some cases, the degree of identification becomes excessive. The child becomes an extension of the parents. When this happens, parents begin to define their own self-worth in terms of their son or daughter's successes or failures. The father who is a "frustrated jock" may seek to experience through his child the success he never knew as an athlete. The parent who was a star may be resentful and rejecting if the child does not attain a similar level of achievement. Some parents thus become "winners" or "losers" through their children, and the pressure placed on the children to excel can be extreme. The child *must* succeed or the parent's self-image is threatened. Much more is at stake than a mere game, and the child of such a parent carries a heavy burden. When parental love and approval depend on how well the child performs, sports are bound to be stressful.

As a coach you might be able to counteract this tendency by explaining the identification process to parents. Tell them that if they place too much pressure on children, they can decrease the potential that sports can have for enjoyment and personal growth. A key to reducing parent-produced stress is to impress on them that youth sports are for young athletes, and that children are not miniature adults. Parents must acknowledge the right of each child to develop athletic potential in an atmosphere that emphasizes participation, personal growth, and fun.

To contribute to the success of your program, parents must be willing and able to commit themselves in many different ways. The following questions can serve as thought-provoking reminders of the scope of parent responsibilities. Parents should be able to honestly answer "yes" to each one.

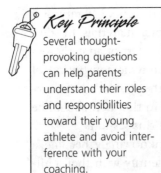

Key Principle

Several thought-provoking questions can help parents understand their roles and responsibilities toward their young athlete and avoid interference with your coaching.

1. *Can the parents give up their child?* This requires putting the child in your charge and trusting you to guide his or her sport experience. Part of this requirement involves accepting your authority and the fact that you may gain some of the admiration and affection that the child once directed solely at his or her parents. This responsibility does not mean that parents cannot have input. But as the coach, you are the boss! If parents are going to undermine your leadership, everyone concerned is going to have problems.

2. *Can the parents admit their shortcomings?* Parents must be convinced that the proper response to a mistake or not knowing something is an honest disclosure. For example, if their child asks a question about sports and they do not know the answer, they should not be afraid to admit it. An honest response is better than a wrong answer. Coaches and parents alike should show children that they realistically accept whatever limitations they have. Surely nobody is perfect, but sometimes children do not learn this because adults fail to teach them.

3. *Can the parents accept their child's triumphs?* Every child athlete experiences "the thrill of victory and the agony of defeat" as part of the competition process. Accepting a child's triumphs sounds easy, but it is not always so. Fathers, in particular, may be competitive with their sons. For example, if a boy does well in a contest, his father may point out minor mistakes, describe how others did even better, or remind his son of even more impressive sport achievements of his own.

4. *Can the parents accept their child's disappointments?* In addition to accepting athletic accomplishments, parents are called upon to support their children when they are disappointed and hurt. This may mean watching them lose a contest while others emerge victorious, or it may mean not being embarrassed, ashamed, or angry when their son or daughter cries after losing. When an apparent disappointment occurs, parents should be able to help their children see the positive side of the situation. Just as competent coaches can change a child's disap-

pointment into self-acceptance, so can parents. Emphasizing effort rather than outcome can be an important means to this goal.

5. *Can the parents give their child some time?* Most programs require a commitment of time, and parents need to decide how much they are willing and able to give. Unfortunately some parents are too busy to become involved. Often this neglect becomes a source of frustration to both parents and children alike. The best advice you can give parents is never to promise more time than they can actually deliver. Recommend that they ask their children about their sport experiences and make every effort to watch some of their contests.

6. *Can the parents let their child make his or her own decisions?* One of the opportunities that sports provide is the chance for children to acquire and practice adult behaviors. An important part of growing up is accepting responsibility for one's own behavior and decisions. This can become a real challenge for parents, because once they invite their child to make decisions, they must support and live with those decisions. Therefore you should encourage parents to provide suggestions and guidance about sports. But ultimately, within reasonable limits, they should let their child athlete become more independent and self-reliant. All parents have ambitions for their child, but they must accept the fact that they cannot dominate the child's life. Sports can offer parents an introduction to the major process of letting go.

7. *Can the parents show their child self-control?* Parents are significant role models for their children in all aspects of life, including sports. It is not surprising to find that parents who exhibit poor self-control in their own lives often have children who are prone to emotional outbursts and poor self-discipline. If parents expect sportsmanship and self-control from their children, they need to exhibit the same qualities in their own behavior.

As part of their responsibilities, parents should watch their children compete in sports. Fortunately, the majority of parents behave appropriately at youth sport events. But the minority who misbehave can spoil it for all the rest. It takes only a few inconsiderate parents to turn what should be a pleasant atmosphere into one that is stressful for all concerned.

Key Principle

Acceptable standards for spectator behavior should be firmly communicated to parents for the purpose of preventing problems at competitive events.

Coaches, program directors, sport officials, and the athletes themselves have a right to demand that spectators conform to acceptable standards of behavior. In addition to acknowledging some obviously inppropriate actions (using profanity, drinking alcohol, throwing objects, etc.), the following rules for parental behavior have been recommended by youth sport authorities:

- Don't interfere with the coach. Parents must be willing to relinquish the responsibility for their child to the coach for the duration of the practice or game.
- Don't shout instructions or criticisms to the children.
- Do remain in the spectator area during the event.
- Don't make abusive comments to athletes, parents, officials, or coaches of either team.
- Do express interest, encouragement, and support to your child.
- Do lend a hand when a coach or official asks for help.

What about parents who violate the rules of conduct? When parents misbehave, it is the duty of other parents and league administrators to step in and correct the situation. It is not your job! You have a huge responsibility in taking care of the team and cannot be expected to police the spectators as well.

Fostering Open Communication with Parents

There is a difference between genuine concern for one's child and disruptive meddling or interference. Parents have both the right and the responsibility to inquire about *all* activities that their children are involved in, including sports. They should take this responsibility seriously, probing into the nature and the quality of specific sport programs. By so doing, they are not being overly protective or showing a lack of confidence in you or your program. Rather, they are fulfilling a child-rearing obligation to oversee the welfare of their loved one.

Key Principle

Communication is the key to friendly, productive relations with parents.

Tell parents of your willingness to discuss any problems that might arise. Let them know that you are open to receiving their input. Also, remember that productive exchange cannot occur unless there is an atmosphere of mutual respect and courtesy.

If you keep the lines of communication open, you will be more likely to have constructive relations with parents. There is, however, a proper time and place for interaction with you. That time is not during practice or a contest, and it is never in the presence of the youngsters. Tell parents what times and places are best suited for discussions with you.

Certain children may have specific characteristics that you should know about. For example, they may have medical or psychological problems that could affect their participation. Encourage parents to share this type of information with you on a confidential basis. This will help prepare you to deal more effectively with the young athlete, and perhaps with the parents as well.

Perhaps the most common cause of coach-parent conflicts is a difference of opinions about the young athlete's abilities. In this regard, the use of a performance measurement system (described in Chapter 5) not only provides valuable feedback to athletes but can be an objective source of performance evaluation for parents. Nevertheless, sometimes parents will disagree with what you are doing as a coach. The main thing is not to get defensive. Even if you do not agree, you can at least *listen* and evaluate the message. You might find some of their suggestions helpful. In the end, however, *you* are the coach and have the final say. Remember that no coach can please everyone. No one can ask any more than what you ask of your athletes—doing the very best job you can and always looking for ways to improve.

Dealing with "Problem Parents"

Key Principle
There are effective ways of dealing with disinterested, overcritical, excessively vocal, meddling, and overprotective parents.

Most parents are enthusiastic and have a true concern for their children. Sometimes, however, parents simply do not realize the trouble they are causing. Instead of being angry with them, recognize that they have a problem, one that you can help solve. Your task is to point out to these people, tactfully and diplomatically, the negative influences of their actions and to encourage them to become more constructive and helpful. Some common types of "problem parents" are described below, and recommendations are included for dealing with them.

Disinterested Parents

Distinguishing characteristics. The most noticeable characteristic of disinterested parents is their absence from team activities to a degree that is upsetting to their child.

What you should do. Talk to the child and ask if the lack of parental involvement troubles her or him. Try to find out why the parents do not participate and contribute, and let them know that you'd welcome their involvement. Make sure that you avoid the mistake of misjudging parents who are actually interested but have good reasons (work, sickness) for missing activities. Explaining the value of sports and how they can draw children and parents closer together may provide parents with a new interest in the activities of their children. In this situation athletes who are not getting enough from their parents may profit from a little extra attention from you. Encourage them; show that you are really interested in them as people.

Overcritical Parents

Distinguishing characteristics. Overcritical parents often scold and berate their child. Such parents are never quite satisfied with their child's performance. They give the impression that it is more "their" experience than it is the athlete's.

What you should do. As discussed earlier, some parents unconsciously equate the success or failure of their child with their own success or failure. As a result they are often hard on their child. You should attempt to make overcritical parents aware of this problem as tactfully as possible. Explain how constant criticism can cause stress and emotional turmoil for their youngster—irritation that actually hinders performance. Tell them why you prefer to use praise and encouragement to motivate and instruct young people, and how parents can do the same.

What you can say. "Mr. Knight, I know you're only trying to help

Billy, but when you criticize him, he gets so nervous that he plays worse, and that certainly takes any fun out of it for him." Or "Mr. Knight, I've found that Billy responds much better to encouragement and praise than he does to criticism. If you were to encourage your son instead of criticizing him so much, sports would be a lot more enjoyable for both of you. After all, it's the kids' game. They play for fun, and too much criticism spoils it for them."

Parents Who Scream from Behind the Bench

Distinguishing characteristics. Some parents seem to have "leather lungs" and large vocal chords. They often sit directly behind the bench, which makes them a distinct danger to the well-being of your eardrums. They frequently rant and rave and virtually drown out everyone else speaking in the area, including you. Everyone is the target for their verbal abuse—team members, opponents, coaches, officials.

What you should do. Do not get into an argument with a screaming parent. It will not do any good and will probably make things worse. During a break in the contest (half time, between periods), ask other parents or league administrators to calmly and tactfully point out to the person that such yelling is a poor example for the young athletes. Ask other people to help out by working with such a person. Also, you can give the disruptive parent a job that will help the team (scouting opponents, keeping stats, looking after equipment). This may provide a greater sense of responsibility and help the screamer to keep quiet.

What you can say. "I know it's easy to get excited, but these kids are out here to have a good time. Try not to take the game so seriously, OK?" Or "Listen, why don't we get together after the game and you can give me some of your ideas on coaching. I'd rather have them afterward because during the game, they're very confusing."

Sideline Coaches

Distinguishing characteristics. Parents who assume the role of sideline coaches are often found leaning over the bench making suggestions to athletes. They may contradict your instructions and disrupt the team.

What you should do. Again, do not confront such a parent right away. Advise your athletes that during practices and contests you are the coach and that you want their full attention. Listening to instructions from others may become confusing. Tell the parent privately how confusing it is for the athletes when two or more people are telling them what to do. You might ask the parent to be either a full-time assistant coach or a full-time spectator.

What you can say. "Mrs. O'Brien, I appreciate your concern and enthusiasm for the team. But when you are coaching Pam from the sidelines, it becomes confusing and distracting to her, especially if I've told her something different. I know you've got some good ideas, and I want to hear them. But please, after the game."

Overprotective Parents

Distinguishing characteristics. Most often the overprotective parents are the mothers of the athletes. Such parents are characterized by their worried looks and comments whenever their son or daughter is playing. Overprotective parents frequently threaten to remove their child because of the dangers involved in the sport.

What you should do. You must try to eliminate the fear of injury by reassuring the parent that the event is fairly safe. Explain the rules and equipment that protect the athlete. Point out how good coaching, program administration, and officiating add to the safety of the sport.

What you can say. "Mrs. Jones, we try to make the game as safe as possible for the athletes. You've got to remember that I wouldn't be coaching kids if I didn't care about them or if I thought the sport was dangerous for them." Or "Mrs. Jones, I care about each one of these kids, and I would never let any of them do anything that I thought would endanger them."

Avoiding Problems with a Preseason Parent Meeting

As a coach, you unselfishly devote a tremendous amount of time and effort to providing a worthwhile life experience for youngsters. All too often you are asked to do "just one more thing." However, successful coaches are aware of the importance of securing the aid and support of

Key Principle

Having a preseason sport orientation meeting is one of the best ways to establish productive relationships with parents and is a good investment for everyone.

well-informed parents. Rather than facing the task of dealing with individual "problem parents" later on, a preseason meeting can be a key to reducing the chance of unpleasant experiences. In other words, having a coach-parent meeting is well worth the additional time and effort!

This part of the chapter is a *guide* for planning and conducting effective coach-parent meetings. Because each coach is unique, it is recommended that you evaluate the information and suggestions and make modifications to suit your personal situation.

Purposes of the Meeting

The overall objective of a coach-parent meeting is to improve parents' understanding of youth sports and what you are trying to accomplish. The following are some more specific purposes:

- To enable parents to become acquainted with you.

- To educate parents about the objectives of youth sports and clarify the goals of your program.

- To inform parents about the specifics of the program and what is expected of the children and parents relative to these details. This includes obtaining parental assistance for accomplishing various tasks and conducting the season's activities.

- To get parents to understand and reinforce the *positive approach* to coaching that you will be using.

- To inform parents about their youth sport obligations and commitments.

- To establish clear lines of communication between you and parents.

- To help you understand the concerns of parents.

A coach-parent meeting might also be used to increase parents' knowledge of the sport. Information about basic rules, skills, and strategies is probably not necessary for the more popular sports, but could be beneficial for the lesser known sports. However, time limitations usually prevent their coverage at a coach-parent meeting. As suggested earlier, part of an early season practice could be devoted to a lecture-demonstration of sport fundamentals. Parents having little background in the sport should be encouraged to attend this session.

Planning and Preparation

One reason for being hesitant about conducting a coach-parent meeting is that you might feel insecure about leading a group of adults. This is not unusual. People are often unwilling to do things for which they have had little training or previous experience. Coaches who have held meetings with parents indicate that it is not an overtaxing experience, and the benefits make the meeting a good investment. The meeting does not have to be elaborate to be successful. However, the importance of being well prepared and organized cannot be over-emphasized!

> *Key Principle*
> With sufficient planning and preparation, a preseason coach-parent meeting can be an enjoyable experience.

1. *When should the meeting be held?* Schedule the meeting early in the season, preferably a week to ten days before the first practice. A weeknight or Saturday morning is probably most convenient. This can be determined by talking with several parents to learn of their preference for the day, time, and place of a meeting.

2. *Where should the meeting be held?* Ideally, your league or club will have a central facility that could be used. If not, the location you select should be easily accessible and should have a meeting room of adequate size, with appropriate features (seating, lighting). If necessary, solicit the assistance of parents. For example, a business person might have access to a company conference room, a teacher might be able to secure the use of a school room, or a service club member might have use of the club facility.

3. *How long should the meeting be?* It will take approximately 1 hour and 15 minutes to cover the necessary topics. It is your responsibility to start the meeting on time, keep it moving along, and finish reasonably close to the specified time.

4. *Should athletes attend the meeting?* Some coaches have no objection to having athletes attend the meeting with their parents. They believe it helps improve communication among all those involved. Other coaches find it more productive to conduct the meeting without the athletes present. Your personal preference will determine the policy adopted. However, if you elect to exclude the athletes, make special arrangements for parents who might not be able to attend without their children. For example, an additional room might be sought in which the children could be shown an educational sport film under the supervision of an assistant coach.

5. *How should parents be informed about the meeting?* Use a personal letter of invitation to notify parents. This letter should be sent at least a week before the meeting date. Include brief statements about the objectives of the meeting, its importance, and the parents' responsibility for attending. Also include information about the date, time, location and directions, attendance by youngsters, and other specifics that you feel are necessary. Send a team roster, including addresses and telephone numbers, with the letter.

As an additional way of promoting attendance, follow-up telephone calls before the meeting are recommended. This could be accomplished by enlisting the aid of parents to set up a chain-calling system.

6. *How can the content be organized?* Provide parents with a written program outline. A carefully prepared outline improves the organizational quality of the meeting, and it helps parents to understand the content. Following an outline makes it easier for you to keep the meeting moving in a crisp, systematic way. This serves to avoid wasteful time lags.

7. *What other preparation is necessary?* Part of the meeting will consist of a question-and-answer session. To prepare yourself for the kinds of questions that might be asked, a booklet entitled *Sports and Your Child* is an excellent source (for pricing and ordering information contact Warde Publishers, 1-800-699-2733).

As an additional consideration, you might want to provide name tags and a sheet on which parents can write their names, addresses, and telephone numbers. Name tags are a good way to learn identities, and they promote the friendly environment that is necessary for a successful meeting. Finally, having refreshments before and after the meeting (coffee and doughnuts, juice) is an effective way to promote interaction among the parents.

Content and Conduct of the Meeting

For any educational program, even the best content is of doubtful value if a cooperative learning environment is not established by the program leader, or if hostility and resistance are created by the participants. If you conduct your meeting as a two-way sharing of information, defensiveness and ill will can be minimized. Some of the parents in attendance will have a considerable amount of knowledge about sports. It is best to take advantage of their expertise by encouraging them to share it with the group.

As the leader of the session, you will do most of the talking. However, the meeting will be more effective if you involve the parents in a discussion, instead of lecturing to them. You can do this by (a) encouraging parents to ask questions, and (b) directing questions to them from time to time and relating their answers to the main points you want to make. Also, in creating an open atmosphere for exchange, it is very important to show respect for the parents. Make them feel that they are a contributing part of the meeting, rather than a mere audience.

The coach-parent meeting described below contains seven separate components. The following program elements are included: (a) opening, (b) objectives of youth sports, (c) details of your sport program, (d) coaching roles and relationships, (e) parent obligations and commitments, (f) coach-parent relations, and (g) closing.

Key Principle

Effective communication is a two-way street, requiring both speaking and listening skills.

Opening (5 minutes). Begin the meeting by introducing yourself and your assistant coach(es). During the welcome, let the parents know that you appreciate their interest and concern. Some parents may not

care enough to attend, but those who do attend deserve credit. In prais-
ing their dedication, point out that they are taking an important step
toward assuring a quality sport experience for their children.

In order to gain the parents' respect, your credibility must be established. You can do this by giving pertinent background information
about your experience in the sport, your experience as a coach, and
special training that you have had, such as attendance at coaching
workshops and clinics. Let them know you are a competent coach, and
that you will make every effort to provide a positive sport experience
by doing the best job you can.

During this introductory period, identify the purposes of the
meeting. In addition, you might want to
invite parents to attend an early practice
session. This will serve to provide them with
information about fundamentals of the
sport. It will also familiarize them with your
coaching style.

Key Principle

Use the meeting as an
opportunity to establish
you personal concern
and credibility as a
coach.

A note of caution is in order. You might
be conducting a coach-parent meeting for
the first time, or might have little experience in leading adults. Do not
begin the meeting by announcing this as a personal shortcoming, or
by asking for the parents' tolerance. Such statements may reduce their
trust and support in you as their child's coach. Self-degrading remarks
may also cause parents to question your ability to conduct the meeting. To gain respect, you must show confidence in leading the session.

Objectives of youth sports (10 minutes). After the opening remarks,
there should be a discussion of the objectives of children's athletics,
including a healthy philosophy of winning (see Chapter 2). Focus on
those goals that are a major part of your coaching. Also, find out which
objectives the parents would like to have emphasized. As pointed out
earlier, if coaches and parents work together to reduce misunderstand-
ings, the objectives can be achieved.

Details of your sport program (10 minutes). During this part of the
meeting, present details about the operation of your sport program. In
addition to other items that you might think of, give consideration to
the following:

- Equipment needed and where it can be purchased.
- Sites and schedules for practices and contests.
- Length of practices and contests.
- Team travel plans.
- Major team rules and guidelines.
- Special rule modifications to be used at this level of competition.
- Medical examinations.
- Insurance.
- Fund-raising projects.
- Communication system for cancellations, etc.
- Midseason and postseason events.

You should also provide information about what is expected of the athletes and parents relative to the program details. Some coaches find it useful to organize a parent committee, giving this committe the task of coordinating parent involvement in many activities of the season.

Coaching roles and relationships (10 minutes). Parents will benefit from knowing about your coaching style. In addition to describing the *positive approach* that you will be using (see Chapter 4), encourage parents to use this approach in interactions with their children.

Key Principle

A key objective is to help parents understand, support, and participate in the positive approach that you will be using with their youngsters.

Parent obligations and commitments (20 minutes). Informing parents about their roles in youth sports and the responsibilities you expect them to fulfill is the most important part of the meeting. Discuss the following topics, which were covered earlier in this chapter:

- Counseling children about sports selection and the level of competition at which they want to play—conferring with and listening to them.
- Dangers of overidentification by parents with their children—the negative impact of this process.
- Parent commitments—the seven important questions to which parents must be able to honestly answer "yes."

- Rules for parent behavior at contests—as the coach, you are responsible for the team, and as parents, they are responsible for their own behavior.

Coach-parent relations (5 minutes). Tell parents of your willingness to discuss any problems that might arise—remember, two-way communication! You should let them know what times and places are best suited for discussions with you.

Closing (20 to 30 minutes). Conclude the meeting with a question-answer session. For this to be worthwhile, you must be ready to cover a wide range of parents' concerns. As indicated earlier, your preparation is best accomplished by reading *Sports and Your Child*. A major part of the manual provides brief answers to the most frequently asked questions about youth sports.

There is an effective technique for starting a question-and-answer period. You can take the lead in raising questions. Stimulate parent involvement by asking the first few questions, and then guide the discussion. If you do not know the answer to a question, do not be ashamed to admit it. The parents will appreciate your honesty. Rather than giving a weak or incorrect response, indicate that it is a question to which you can both seek an answer. Perhaps someone in the audience will be able to provide the answer. Do not give the impression that every question must be addressed and answered by you.

> *Key Principle*
> Coaches can serve as a valuable source of sport information for parents.

You might want to take some time to assess the format and content of the meeting and your style of presentation. Evaluative comments might be solicited from parents through informal discussion. Feedback can be valuable for making changes to improve the quality of future meetings. Finally, at the end of the meeting, do not forget to thank the parents again for attending.

The coach-parent meeting is a vitally important tool for developing parent involvement and support. A successful meeting will help solidify the athletic triangle (coach-athlete-parent) and lead to positive youth sport experiences.

What to Do If. . .

The successful person is one who finds an opportunity in every problem. Unsuccessful people find a problem in every opportunity.

Lou Holtz, college football coach

During our Coach Effectiveness Training workshops, we always allocate a period of time for discussion of challenging issues and situations that the coaches themselves have encountered. Over the years, certain critical issues have surfaced repeatedly, suggesting that there is a good chance that you, too, might have to deal with one or more of them. In this final chapter, we present common problems and recommendations for solving them.

Gaining Athletes' Respect

Regardless of the level at which you are coaching, gaining the respect of the athletes is critical for increasing their receptiveness to your skill instruction, maintaining discipline, and developing team cohesiveness. But how is such respect gained? Is it through a "tough guy" approach that affirms your control over them and creates distance between yourself and the athletes? This does work in some ways, but taken to an extreme, it can reduce the quality of interaction and enjoyment of the activity.

Obviously, you have to establish your role as the leader, the person in charge. On the other hand, you don't need to be Attila the Hun to gain respect. You can provide the firm structure that young athletes want and need within the context of a *positive* coaching approach. Numerous interviews with young athletes about what they liked and did not like about their coaches' behaviors suggest four keys to gaining such respect:

- Show your athletes that you can teach them to develop their skills and that you are willing to make the effort to do so.

- Establish team rules early (preferably with athlete input) and firmly yet fairly enforce them. No special deals for stars; they should be treated no more preferentially than your benchwarmers.

- Be a fair and considerate leader. Show them that you care about them as individuals and that you are glad to be coaching them.

- Set a good example by showing respect for yourself, for your athletes, and for others—opponents, parents, officials. You cannot demand respect. True respect must be earned.

Should Kids Ever Be Cut?

Heartbreak can be experienced when youngsters are eliminated from sports participation. Surely not all children can be on the team of their choosing, but we believe that every youngster should have a chance to play. Prior to the age of 14, the practice of cutting children from sport programs is indefensible. At the high school level it is appropriate to have select leagues to allow gifted athletes to develop their skills. But even at this age, alternative programs should be available for less-talented youngsters who wish to play the sport.

The tragedy of cutting children from sport programs lies in the fact that those cut are almost always the least skilled or those who have discipline problems. It is precisely these children who are in need of an opportunity to grow through sport. Here again, we must choose between a professional model and one devoted to the development of children.

What should you do if you must cut a youngster? The first thing is to realize that whether or not the athlete shows it, he or she is likely to feel disappointed, rejected—and perhaps even humiliated. The youngster needs your support at this very difficult time. You can give support by acknowledging the disappointment felt by the child. Do not tell the child not to be disappointed or make unrealistic excuses for why it happened. All people must learn to face disappointments in life. You can make this easier if you show that your personal regard for her or him has not diminished.

In addition to communicating your understanding, you may be able to suggest options in other programs in the same sport or in other sports. One child who was at first devastated by being cut from a peewee football team was helped by his coach to get involved in a soccer program and is now having a great time.

What If a Child Wants to Quit?

At one time or another, and for a variety of reasons, most athletes think about quitting. Sometimes a decision to quit comes as a shock to the coach, but at other times the warning signs leading up to the decision are very clear.

What are the causes of dropping out of youth sports? In general, the reasons fall into two categories. The first category involves a shift in interests, especially in adolescents. Other involvements, such as a job, a boyfriend or girlfriend, or recreational pursuits may leave little time for sports involvement. In such cases a youngster may simply choose to set other priorities.

The second general set of reasons why youngsters drop out relates to negative sports experiences, such as the following.

- Not getting enough playing time.

- Poor relationships with coaches or teammates.

- An overemphasis on winning that creates stress and reduces fun.

- Overorganization, excessive repetition, and regimentation leading to boredom.

- Excessive fear of failure, including frustration or failure to achieve personal or team goals.

If the youngster has decided that other activities are more important, his or her priorities should be respected. However, it is wise to provide a reminder that a commitment has been made to the program and to teammates and that athletes owe it to themselves and to others to honor commitments and to finish out the season. This gives the youngster an opportunity to feel good about himself or herself by fulfilling the obligation through the rest of the season—even if the activity itself is no longer pleasurable.

If the decision to quit is based on one or more of the negative factors listed above, there is a legitimate problem that needs to be addressed by you, the coach. These problems are far less likely to occur when the Coach Effectiveness Training principles have been applied. Indeed, as our research on dropout has shown, the *positive approach* is the best way to avoid such problems. If athletes begin dropping out, we recommend that you honestly examine your own coaching practices in light of the behavioral guidelines in Chapter 4.

Unusual Disciplinary Problems

In Chapter 11 we discussed approaches to dealing with several classes of "problem athletes." Although they may be a headache for the coach, most problem athletes can be successfully dealt with. Given our emphasis on the benefits of participation and our opposition to cutting athletes, are there ever instances in which an athlete should be expelled from a program?

Unfortunately, there are a few athletes whose behavior is so disruptive or even dangerous to others that the welfare of others must override the concern for the individual. For example, one coach discovered that a team member was offering drugs to other athletes. In another instance, a youngster was subject to uncontrollable violent outbursts against his teammates. Obviously such behaviors cannot and should not be tolerated.

Elimination from a program is a last resort that should occur only after reasonable efforts have been made to correct the problem. The situation is complicated by the fact that sports may be the only medium for reaching the child, and your relationship with the youngster may turn out to be a curative one for a child from a bad home situation.

If you encounter an especially severe disciplinary problem, the first step may be a conference with the parent(s) to see if they can help. In some extreme cases, referral to a professional counselor may allow the child to remain in the program, and continued participation can be used to motivate change. In any event, it is not your responsibility as a coach to shoulder the burden alone, and it is not fair to subject your other athletes to intolerable situations. You have plenty to do as a coach; do not hesitate to seek outside assistance.

Dealing with a Tough Loss or Losing Streak

Children differ a great deal in their reactions to a loss. Some may be barely affected or may forget the loss almost immediately. Others will be virtually devastated by the loss and may be low-spirited for days. Avoid the temptation to deny or distort what the child is feeling. If one of your players has struck out three times and made an error that lost the game, she does not want to hear "You did great." She knows she didn't, and your attempts to comfort her in this manner may well come through as a lack of understanding about how she feels. Likewise, it is not very helpful to tell a child that "it doesn't matter." The fact is that at that moment it does matter a great deal!

Is there anything you can do to make your athletes feel better without distorting reality? One thing you can do is to point out something positive that was achieved during the contest. A wrestling match may have been lost, but some good takedowns and escapes may have been executed. By emphasizing these accomplishments, you can help your athletes paint a more balanced picture.

Another thing that you can do is to look to the future rather than dwell on the loss. Nothing can be done about the loss, so the most productive view is to focus on what has been learned and can be used to improve future performance.

Above all, don't blame or get angry with the athletes if they have given maximum effort. They feel bad enough already. Support and understanding, sincerely given, will be very helpful at this time. If they haven't given maximum effort, communicate your unhappiness without disparaging them as people. They need to learn that effort is completely controllable and that they are accountable.

Again, focus on the future and tell them that they owe it to themselves and their team to give maximum effort. Effort is a *decision*, not a trait.

Perhaps your team loses regularly. If winning is the only goal that is set, athletes will be constantly frustrated. If, on the other hand, goals focused on effort and improvement are emphasized, a sense of accomplishment can result as improvement occurs, and this can help blunt the disappointments of losing. Knowledgeable coaches often use individual and team goal setting to create a kind of "game within the game." For example, the team objective may be to reduce the number of errors, strikeouts, fumbles, or penalties in the next few games. Even if games are lost, children can experience a sense of accomplishment as they attain modified goals.

You can promote similar goal setting on an individual level with your athletes. In addition to performance goals, you can place emphasis on such important ingredients to success as effort and teamwork. Many a team and many an athlete has been helped to feel as if progress was made toward a larger objective when they succeeded at smaller subgoals.

Dealing with a Winning Streak

Strangely enough, winning can create its own problems. One is overconfidence and the well-known swelled head. Unless carefully handled, winning teams can become arrogant and disrespectful to teams they defeat. And a long winning streak can provide pressures of its own when the emphasis becomes the outcome rather than the process of competition.

Youngsters should be allowed to feel good about winning—they've earned it. But they should also be reminded to show consideration for their opponents. Emphasize that it never feels good to lose and there is no justification for rubbing it in. Instead, tell youngsters to be gracious winners and to give their opponents a pat on the back or a handshake in a sincere manner. Remind them that their opponents make it possible for them to enjoy the process of competing.

During a winning streak, most athletes experience not only the pleasure of winning but also the increased pressure not to lose (especially when the parents jump on the band wagon). An additional danger is that if a team wins too regularly and too easily, they may get bored and take their success for granted. A focus on effort and continued improvement can provide an additional and meaningful goal for youngsters. It is important to communicate that you expect continual striving for victory. Again, winning is to be sought, but it is not the only objective. Finally, don't allow your athletes to rest on past laurels. Point out that past success does not constitute a guarantee of no mistakes or losses in the future.

Trophies and Other Awards

Children usually participate in sports because of their intrinsic motivation to play "for the fun of it." What happens when material or extrinsic awards, such as money and large trophies, are introduced as an additional reward for winning? Can they lose their intrinsic motivation? Sadly, the answer is yes.

If carried to an extreme, external rewards can replace intrinsic motivation as the reason for participating in sports. When the young athletes begin to see these extrinsic rewards as the reason for their participation, the removal of these rewards may result in a loss of interest in participation.

An unhappy example of exactly this effect is the case of a teenage wrestler whose father called one of us. The father was very concerned because his young athlete refused to enter meets unless the winners' trophies were large enough to justify competing.

We are not suggesting that trophies and other extrinsic rewards be eliminated from sports. They certainly have their rightful place as a means of recognizing outstanding effort and achievement. It is important, however, that adults and children maintain a proper perspective so that trophies do not become the be-all and end-all of participation. It is sad indeed when children lose the capacity to enjoy athletic competition for its own sake. Make sure the awards are of modest proportion, and be sure to have awards for the most-improved and dedicated player, as well as the most skillful one.

Misbehavior by Other Coaches

Some of the knottiest problems that arise in youth sports involve relationships with other coaches. Sometimes, coaches witness unacceptable behavior by other coaches that could have serious negative consequences for youngsters. The tricky part comes in deciding whether it is appropriate for you to be involved. When does appropriate concern become interfering and meddling? What should you do if issues like the following crop up?

• The coach is mistreating youngsters either verbally or physically.

• The coach is engaging in inappropriate behavior, such as bad language or hazing of officials or opponents.

• The coach is using technically incorrect, questionable, or possibly dangerous coaching methods.

• The coach is losing perspective on the purpose of youth sports and seems preoccupied with winning, thus putting additional stress on athletes.

Because each situation is somewhat unique, there are no cut-and-dried answers that apply to every case. Nonetheless, there are some general principles that can be helpful in approaching and resolving such problems.

When incidents such as those listed above occur, it would be a mistake not to consider them problems. As uncomfortable as it may be to either confront or report another coach, we must never lose sight of the primary focus—the welfare of the children.

If you have a personal relationship with the coach that will permit you to approach him or her with your concerns, this can be a useful avenue to resolving the problem. On the other hand, it may be necessary to express your concerns to the program administrators, whose responsibility it is to take the appropriate remedial actions.

Coaching Your Own Child

Many volunteer coaches find their way into youth sport programs because their own son or daughter is participating. Therefore the majority of coaches end up coaching their own child at one time or another. This often results in confusion as to how to deal with the dual roles of coach and parent.

Experienced coaches who have faced this challenge have found a number of principles to be useful. First of all, you and your child need to be aware that your behavior when you are coaching will have to be different than how you behave at home. You now have a responsibility not only to your child, but to all of the other young athletes as well. Recognizing this fact, here are some principles you can follow:

- Ask your child how he or she feels about having you for a coach. Does the child fear undue pressure in the form of either perceived favoritism or excessive demands? If so, give reassurance that you will be fair and impartial and that no more or less will be expected of him or her. Knowing how your child feels will help guide your decision concerning whether your child should be on your team.

- Discuss with your child how your role will change when you are in the athletic environment, and why you need to treat him or her like any other team member.

- Be a parent at home and a coach on the field or court. Make sure that your separate roles are clear in your mind and in your child's.

- Above all, demonstrate in your words and actions that your love for your child does not depend on his or her athletic performance.

Coaching and Family Life

As you are well aware, coaching is very time consuming and takes a lot of energy. Many families find that practices are held during the dinner hour and that their kitchen has become a cafeteria with several shifts. The fun and togetherness of family meals can become a thing of the past. For most families, this is only a seasonal happening. But for coaches who have year-round involvements, it becomes the normal pattern of living. Spouses and children can begin to feel neglected.

When you agree to coach, be aware of what is likely to be required and how much time and effort you are willing to devote. Once into a program, you should also keep in mind that you can easily be seduced into more and more involvement. Before you know it, coaching responsibilities can snowball into a second career, with too little time remaining for your family responsibilities.

Find ways to spend adequate time with your children, particularly those who are not involved in sports. Likewise, it is important for spouses to devote time to their own relationship. For couples who have children, private moments spent away from the children can serve to maintain and invigorate their marriage. Recreational pursuits for you and your spouse, an occasional weekend away by yourselves, dinners out, and a cultivation of interests you share in common can help maintain the sparkle in your marriage.

A Final Word

In this section of the book, we have focused on some of the challenges and negatives of coaching. However, as we ourselves have learned through our coaching experiences, the positives greatly outweigh the negatives. Every problem athlete, problem parent, and coaching headache is outweighed by the moments of satisfaction that come from helping young athletes grow socially, athletically, and personally. Our own children's lives have been enriched by their youth sport experiences. Although most coaches do not get the credit they rightfully deserve, we know full well that they do indeed make important contributions to the lives of children. And so, our final words are,

Way to go, Coach!

References

General Resources

Nygaard, G., & Boone, T. H. (1985). *Coaches guide to sport law.* Champaign, IL: Human Kinetics.

Sawyer, T. H. (1992). Legal issues in coaching. In V. Seefeldt & E. W. Brown (Eds.), *Program for athletic coaches' education.* Dubuque, IA: Brown & Benchmark.

Smith, R. E. (2001). Positive reinforcement, performance feedback, and performance enhancement. In J. M. Williams (Ed.), *Applied sport psychology: Personal growth to peak performance,* 4th ed., pp. 29-42. Mountain View, CA: Mayfield.

Smith, R. E., & Smoll, F. L. (1997). Coach-mediated team building in youth sports. *Journal of Applied Sport Psychology, 9,* 114-132.

Smith, R. E., & Smoll, F. L. (1997). Coaching the coaches: Youth sports as a scientific and applied behavioral setting. *Current Directions in Psychological Science, 6,* 16-21.

Smith, R. E., & Smoll, F. L., & Christensen, D. S. (1996). Behavioral assessment and interventions in youth sports. *Behavior Modification, 20,* 3-44.

Smoll, F. L. (2001). Coach-parent relationships in youth sports: Increasing harmony and minimizing hassle. In J. M. Williams (Ed.), *Applied sport psychology: Personal growth to peak performance,* 4th ed., pp. 150-161. Mountain View, CA: Mayfield.

Smoll, F. L., & Smith, R. E. (1997). *Coaches who never lose: Making sure athletes win, no matter what the score.* Portola Valley, CA: Warde.

Smoll, F. L., & Smith, R. E. (1999). *Sports and your child: A 50-minute guide for parents.* Portola Valley, CA: Warde.

Smoll, F. L., & Smith, R. E. (2001). Conducting sport psychology training programs for coaches: Cognitive-behavioral principles and techniques. In J. M. Williams (Ed.), *Applied sport psychology: Personal growth to peak performance*, 4th ed., pp. 378-400. Mountain View, CA: Mayfield.

Smoll, F. L., & Smith, R. E. (Eds.). (2001). *Children and youth in sport: A biopsychosocial perspective* (2nd ed.). Dubuque, IA: Kendall/Hunt.

Research Articles Related to Coach Effeciveness Training

Barnett, N. P., Smoll, F. L., & Smith, R. E. (1992). Effects of enhancing coach-athlete relationships on youth sport attrition. *The Sport Psychologist, 6*, 111-127.

Curtis, B., Smith, R. E., & Smoll, F. L. (1979). Scrutinizing the skipper: A study of leadership behaviors in the dugout. *Journal of Applied Psychology, 64*, 391-400.

Smith, R. E., & Smoll, F. L. (1990). Self-esteem and children's reactions to youth sport coaching behaviors: A field study of self-enhancement processes. *Developmental Psychology, 26*, 987-993.

Smith, R. E., Smoll, F. L., & Barnett, N. P. (1995). Reduction of children's sport performance anxiety through social support and stress-reduction training for coaches. *Journal of Applied Developmental Psychology, 16*, 125-142.

Smith, R. E., Smoll, F. L., & Curtis, B. (1978). Coaching behaviors in Little League Baseball. In F. L. Smoll & R. E. Smith (Eds.), *Psychological perspectives in youth sports*, pp. 173-201. Washington, DC: Hemisphere.

Smith, R. E., Smoll, F. L., & Curtis, B. (1979). Coach effectiveness training: A cognitive-behavioral approach to enhancing relationship skills in youth sport coaches. *Journal of Sport Psychology, 1*, 59-75.

Smith, R. E., Smoll, F. L., & Hunt, E. B. (1977). A system for the behavioral assessment of athletic coaches. *Research Quarterly, 48*, 401-407.

Smith, R. E., Zane, N. W. S., Smoll, F. L., & Coppel, D. B. (1983). Behavioral assessment in youth sports: Coaching behaviors and children's attitudes. *Medicine and Science in Sports and Exercise, 15*, 208-214.

Smoll, F. L., & Smith, R. E. (1989). Leadership behaviors in sport: A conceptual model and research paradigm. *Journal of Applied Social Psychology, 19*, 1522-1551.

Smoll, F. L., Smith, R. E., Barnett, N. P., & Everett, J. J. (1993). Enhancement of children's self-esteem through social support training for youth sport coaches. *Journal of Applied Psychology, 78*, 602-610.

Smoll, F. L., Smith, R. E., Curtis, B., & Hunt, E. (1978). Toward a mediational model of coach-player relationships. *Research Quarterly, 49*, 528-541.

*Coach's
Clipboard*

A summary of Key Principles from
Way to Go, Coach!

Part I
Developing a Coaching Philosophy

1. ***Key Principle:*** **A realistic appraisal of youth sports acknowledges both their benefits and the potential harm that can be done when programs are not properly structured and supervised. The key is to improve the quality of experiences for all youngsters.**

   Coaching Strategy: Perhaps the key to unlocking the potential of youth sports lies in being well informed about their psychological dimensions. The guidelines presented in this book are designed to assist you in your role as a successful coach.

2. ***Key Principle:*** **Sportsmanship is taught not only by verbalizing moral principles but also by serving as a positive role model. In teaching moral values, what coaches do is as important as what they say.**

   Coaching Strategy: Coaches can behave in ways that teach either morality or immorality. For example, by trying to get the edge by stretching the rules, coaches can easily give children the impression that cheating is not really wrong unless it is detected, and then only to the extent that it hurts the chances of winning. When coaches bend the rules in order to obtain a victory, children may conclude that the end justifies the means. Likewise, coaches who display hostility toward officials and contempt for the other team communicate the notion that such behaviors are appropriate and desirable. Even when coaches preach correct values, it is essential that they themselves behave in accordance with them. Research studies with children have repeatedly shown that when adults' actions are inconsistent with their words, it is the actions, not the words, that influence children's behavior. Actions do indeed speak louder than words.

Coach's Clipboard

3. *Key Principle:* Professional sport is a commercial enterprise in which success is measured in wins and financial revenues.

   Coaching Strategy: In a developmental model, sport is an arena for learning, where success is measured in terms of personal growth and development. Sometimes these two athletic models get confused. Most of the problems in youth sports occur when uninformed adults erroneously impose a professional model on what should be a recreational and educational experience for children.

4. *Key Principle:* Among the many benefits that children can derive from sports, perhaps the most important is simply to have fun.

   Coaching Strategy: Winning adds to the fun, but we sell sports short if we insist that winning is the most important ingredient. In fact, several studies reported that when children were asked where they would rather be—warming the bench on a winning team or playing regularly on a losing team—about 90% of the children chose the losing team. The message is clear: The enjoyment of playing is more important to children than the satisfaction of winning.

5. *Key Principle:* "Success is peace of mind, which is a direct result of self-satisfaction in knowing you did your best to become the best that you are capable of becoming." —John Wooden, former UCLA basketball coach

   Coaching Strategy: Know the four components of the Real Meaning of Winning:
   1. Winning isn't everything, nor is it the only thing.
   2. Failure is not the same thing as losing.
   3. Success is not equivalent to winning.
   4. Children should be taught that success is found in striving for victory. The important idea is that success is related to effort!

Part II

Becoming a Better Coach

6. ***Key Principle:*** **The psychology of coaching is simply a set of strategies designed to increase your ability to influence others positively.**

   Coaching Strategy: It is often said that psychology is the application of common sense. The coaching guidelines presented in the book make good sense. But more important, research has shown them to be effective ways to increase motivation, morale, enjoyment of the athletic situation, and performance.

7. ***Key Principle:*** **The negative approach to coaching is characterized by the use of punishment and criticism to eliminate mistakes. It operates through the creation of fear.**

   Coaching Strategy: Evidence is strong that punishment has certain undesirable side effects. These can actually interfere with what a coach is trying to accomplish. Using too much punishment promotes the development of fear of failure. The athlete with a fear of failure is motivated, not by positive desire to achieve and enjoy the "thrill of victory," but by a fear of "the agony of defeat."

8. ***Key Principle:*** **The positive approach to coaching is designed to increase desirable behaviors and to create positive motivation rather than fear of failing. It has none of the negative side effects of the negative approach.**

   Coaching Strategy: The positive approach, through its emphasis on improving rather than on "not screwing up," fosters a more desirable learning environment and tends to promote more positive relationships among coaches and athletes.

9. ***Key Principle:*** **Coach Effectiveness Training (CET) favorably affects liking for the coach, teammates, and the sport experience. It also increases children's self-esteem, reduces performance anxiety, and counteracts dropout.**

   Coaching Strategy: A one-year follow up study showed a dropout rate of 26% among children who played for untrained coaches, a figure that is quite consistent with previous reports of attrition in youth sports. In contrast, only 5% of the children who had played for CET-trained coaches failed to return to the program the next season!

10. ***Key Principle:*** **The most effective way to build and strengthen desirable behavior is to use your "reinforcement power."**

   Coaching Strategy: Potential reinforcers include social behaviors such as verbal praise, nonverbal signs such as smiles or applause, and physical contact such as a pat on the back. They also include the opportunity to engage in certain activities (such as extra batting practice) or to play with a particular piece of equipment. Social reinforces are most frequently employed in athletics. The best way to find an effective reinforcer is to get to know each athlete's likes and dislikes. In this area it is "different strokes for different folks."

11. ***Key Principle:*** **Successful coaching requires skillful use of reinforcement. Start reinforcing what each athlete is capable of doing, and gradually require more as skills improve.**

   Coaching Strategy: Know the four key principles of reinforcement:
   1. Be liberal with reinforcement.
   2. Have realistic expectations and consistently reinforce achievement.
   3. Give reinforcement for desirable behavior as soon as it occurs.
   4. Reinforce ***effort*** as much as results.

12. ***Key Principle:*** **If you manage things right, mistakes can be golden opportunities to improve performance, for they provide the feedback that is needed to make adjustments.**

   Coaching Strategy: John Wooden referred to mistakes as the "stepping stones to achievement." They provide information that is needed to improve performance. By communicating this concept to athletes in word and action, you can help them accept and learn from their mistakes.

13. *Key Principle:* In giving corrective instruction, don't emphasize the bad effects of the mistake. Instead, point out the good things that will happen if the athlete follows your instruction.

Coaching Strategy: Here are some practical guidelines for reacting to mistakes:
1. Give encouragement immediately after a mistake.
2. If an athlete knows how to correct the mistake, encouragement alone is sufficient.
3. When appropriate, give corrective instruction after a mistake, but always do so in an encouraging and positive way. Use the "positive sandwich" when possible.
   - Start with a compliment for something the athlete did right.
   - Give the future-oriented instruction ("If you follow the ball all the way into your hands, you'll catch those just like a pro does.")
   - End with another positive statement, such as encouragement to keep trying.
4. Don't punish when things go wrong.
5. Don't give corrective instruction in a hostile or punitive way.

14. *Key Principle:* Teaching self-discipline is an important youth sport objective. But it need not be based on punitive control; the positive approach can be applied here as well.

Coaching Strategy: Know the guidelines:
1. Maintain order by establishing clear expectations and a "team rule" concept.
2. Involve athletes in developing the rules and work to build team unity in achieving them.
3. Strive to achieve a balance between freedom and structure.

15. *Key Principle:* Team rules should be developed early in the season.

Coaching Strategy:
1. Explain why team rules are necessary (they keep things organized and efficient, thereby increasing the chances of achieving individual and team objectives.)
2. Explain why the team rules should be something that they can agree on as a group (they will be their rules, and it will be their responsibility to follow them.)
3. Solicit suggestions and ideas, and listen to what athletes say to show that their ideas and feelings are valued.
4. Incorporate athletes' input into a reasonable set of rules. Rules should provide structure and yet not be too rigid.
5. Discuss the kinds of penalties that you will use for breaking team rules.

16. **Key Principle:** Don't take it personally when young athletes violate team rules; it's a natural part of establishing their independence. There are productive ways of dealing with such violations.

Coaching Strategy:
1. Allow the athlete to explain his/her actions.
2. Be consistent and impartial.
3. Don't express anger and a punitive attitude.
4. Don't lecture or embarrass the athlete.
5. Focus on the fact that a team policy has been violated, placing the responsibility on the athlete.
6. When giving penalties, it is best to deprive athletes of something they value.
7. Don't use physical measures that could become aversive by being used to punish (running laps, doing push-ups). *It is not educationally sound to have beneficial physical activities become unpleasant because they have been used as punishment.*

17. **Key Principle:** The positive approach is a proven way to develop team cohesion. This is done by modeling and reinforcing mutually supportive behaviors.

Coaching Strategy:
1. Set a good example of behavior.
2. Encourage effort, don't demand results.
3. In giving encouragement, be selective so that it is meaningful.
4. Never give encouragement or instruction in a sarcastic or degrading manner.
5. Encourage athletes to be supportive of each other, and reinforce them when they do so.

Coach's Clipboard

---

18. *Key Principle:* Teach sport skills effectively.

   Coaching Strategy:
   1. Establish your teaching role as early as possible.
   2. Let your athletes know that a primary coaching goal is to help them develop their athletic potential.
   3. During each practice or contest, be sure that every youngster gets recognized at least once.
   4. Always give instructions positively. Emphasize the good things that will happen if athletes do it right rather than focusing totally on the negative things that will occur if they do not.
   5. When giving instructions, be clear and concise.
   6. Show athletes the correct technique.
   • Introduce a skill with a demonstration.
   • Provide an accurate, but brief verbal explanation.
   • Have athletes actively practice the skill.
   7. Reinforce *effort and progress*. Again, the foundation of the positive approach is giving reinforcement for effort as well as desirable performance and psychosocial behavior.

---

19. *Key Principle:* Awareness of one's own behavior is central to becoming more effective, and such awareness can be increased through feedback and self-monitoring.

   Coaching Strategy: Utilize the Coach Self-Report Form on page 47.

Coach's
Clipboard

Part III

Performance Enhancement Skills for Young Athletes

20. **Key Principle:** Goal setting operates by directing and mobilizing effort, increasing commitment and persistence, and helping people find new and more effective strategies.

Coaching Strategy:

1. Set specific goals in terms that can be measured.
2. Set difficult but realistic goals.
3. Set short-range as well as long-range goals.
4. Set performance goals as opposed to outcome goals.
5. Express goals in positive rather than negative terms.
6. Set goals for both practices and competition.
7. Identify specific goal achievement strategies.
8. Record goals, achievement strategies, and target dates for attaining goals.
9. Set up a performance feedback or goal evaluation system.
10. Goal-setting programs are most effective when they are supported by those individuals who are important in the athlete's life.

21. **Key Principle:** Mental toughness is best viewed as a set of specific, learnable skills that can give a youngster the winning edge not only in sports, but in other life settings as well.

Coaching Strategy: "Mentally tough" athletes view themselves and pressure situations in ways that arouse a positive desire to achieve rather than a fear of failure. Another specific skill that contributes to mental toughness is the ability to keep physical arousal within manageable limits. "Mentally tough" athletes are able to "psych up" with enough arousal to optimize their performance without being "psyched out" by excessive arousal.

Copyright ©2001 Ronald E. Smith and Frank L. Smoll. Published by Warde Publishers, Inc.

22. **Key Principle:** Coaches can be either a source of stress by using the negative approach, or a buffer against its harmful effects by adopting the positive approach of Coach Effectiveness Training.

Coaching Strategy: The first way you can reduce stress is to change aspects of the situation that place unnecessary demands on young athletes. Many young athletes experience unnecessary stress because adults put undue performance pressure on them. It is quite normal to feel insecure when we don't have the skills needed to cope with a situation. Many young athletes experience this insecurity when they first begin to learn a sport. As their athletic skills increase, they become better able to deal with the demands of the athletic situation, and their stress decreases. Thus, being an effective teacher and working with young athletes to improve their skills is one way that you can help reduce athletic stress. When a team can pull together and support one another in pressure situations, this kind of social support can help reduce the level of stress experienced by individual athletes.

23. **Key Principle:** Pressure is not produced by situations but by the way we think about and interpret those situations. Mentally tough competitors manage pressure well largely because they have become disciplined thinkers.

Coaching Strategy: Thoughts like these produce pressure:
- "What if I don't do well?"
- "I can't blow it now."
- "I'll never live it down if I lose."
- "If I miss these free throws, what will everyone say?"
- "If I don't sink this putt, I'll lose everything!"

On the other hand, mentally tough athletes think like this in pressure situations:
- "I'm going to do the best that I can and let the cards fall where they may."
- "All I can do is give 100%. No one can do more."
- "This is supposed to be fun, and I'm going to make sure it is."
- "I don't have to put pressure on myself. All I have to do is focus on doing my job the best I know how."
- "I'm going to focus on the good things that will happen when I make the play."
- "I'm concentrating on performing, rather than winning or losing."

Coach's Clipboard

24. ***Key Principle:*** Mastering coping skills at an early age can benefit a child throughout life, and coaches can teach one of these skills through relaxation training.

   Coaching Strategy: Utilize the relaxation techniques outlined on pages 77-79.

25. ***Key Principle:*** Sport Science research has shown that a combination of physical and mental practice is often more effective than physical practice alone.

   Coaching Strategy: Introduce the power of imagery to athletes. Use the fun activity presented on page 84.

Coach's
Clipboard

Part IV

Health and Safety Considerations

26. *Key Principle:* **Body structure and function are important in determining how satisfying and enjoyable sports can be.**

Coaching Strategy: Help youngsters to select sports and to play positions within a sport that are in harmony with their physical makeup. More exactly, make sure their body size (height and weight), body build (endomorphy, mesomorphy, ectomorphy), and body composition (percentage of bone, muscle, and fat) are compatible with the requirements of the activity. This will give them a better chance for attaining athletic success.

27. *Key Principle:* **If someone wishes to develop the body of an elite athlete and the potential to respond ideally to a sport training program, the individual should select his or her parents with great care.**

Coaching Strategy: Both the structure of the body and the way it responds to exercise and training are in large part determined by heredity, but the effects of genetics are never absolute. Constantly strive to optimize environmental factors that affect young athletes' growth and development (e.g., health, nutrition, and physical activity).

28. *Key Principle:* **Children's exercise tolerance is greater than believed in the past.**

Coaching Strategy: Unfortunately, there is no exact guide for determining how much activity is appropriate. When planning and supervising endurance-training programs, give consideration to:

- The maturation level of the child.
- The frequency and duration of the activity.
- The child's knowledge of his or her limits.

29. *Key Principle:* **Girls are nearer their final body size at any age because they mature at a faster rate than boys.**

Coaching Strategy: Girls are biologically more mature than boys, but sex differences in body structure and motor performance are very slight. Allow prepubescent boys and girls to participate on the same teams competing with and against each other.

30. *Key Principle:* **All boys and girls experience an adolescent growth spurt.**

Coaching Strategy: Because of sex differences in (a) timing of the adolescent growth spurt, (b) the amount of gain that occurs, and (c) hormone levels, there is a great discrepancy in body size and proportions of postpubescent males and females. Consequently, males can be expected to develop greater strength and surpass females in the performance of most sport-related skills. Sex-segregated competition should therefore be provided for postpubescent athletes.

31. *Key Principle:* **For adolescent females, decreased motivation and increased sedentary habits are major causes of lowered performance.**

Coaching Strategy: The so-called female plateau in performance is primarily caused by gender-related attitudes and behaviors, rather than biological changes associated with puberty. To promote continuing improvement in performance, give adolescent females:

- Improved opportunities for sport participation.
- Adequate facilities and equipment.
- High-quality technical instruction.
- Encouragement to excel in sports.

32. *Key Principle:* **After puberty, girls should have separate but equal opportunities for sport participation.**

Coaching Strategy: During adolescence, boys generally become larger and stronger and gain decided physical advantages, which makes mixed-sex competition in most sports unfair and dangerous. After age 11, provide boys and girls with their own competitive opportunities in sports.

33. *Key Principle:* **The growth plate of the young athlete is vulnerable to injury.**

Coaching Strategy: Although the growth plate is the weakest point in the bone, growth-plate injuries are not common in youth sports. Nevertheless, take appropriate safety measures to protect young athletes in collision sports, such as football and wrestling, where severe blows to a leg or arm may be encountered.

Coach's Clipboard

34. *Key Principle:* **The difference in ability level of young athletes is often a result of different maturity levels.**

Coaching Strategy: During grade school and junior high school, the early-maturing boy has physical advantages over his teammates and opponents. He is bigger, stronger, and quicker, acquires sport skills faster, and has more endurance potential than his peers. Learn to recognize the signs of early maturing, and expect the early-maturing boy to be an outstanding athlete.

35. *Key Principle:* **The potential problems of early maturing athletes are fairly easy to avoid.**

Coaching Strategy: When others catch up to him in maturity and ability, the former star's self-esteem may be threatened. To prevent problems from occurring:

1. Identify early maturing youngsters.
2. Provide opportunities for the early-maturing individual to participate in sports with individuals who are of similar maturity, not the same calendar age.
3. Help early-maturing boys to keep their athletic performances and potentials in proper perspective.

36. *Key Principle:* **Late-maturing youngsters need understanding and special attention from coaches and parents alike.**

Coaching Strategy: Late-maturers are likely to be handicapped in many sports where size, strength, and endurance determine the outcome. In some situations, they are subject to greater risk of injury.

1. Consider postponing entry into sport programs until late maturers are physically ready.
2. Know the implications of delayed adolescent development, and develop expectations about performance accordingly.
3. Limit training for strength and endurance during the first two years of high school.
4. Provide liberal amounts of encouragement and support.

37. *Key Principle:* **Children are growing to a larger size and maturing more rapidly than ever before.**

Coaching Strategy: Adjust sport programs and coaching expectations to accommodate accelerated maturity and higher levels of athletic performance. Moreover, provide a higher degree of sophistication in dealing with a variety of concerns, such as protective equipment, training practices, and coaching styles.

Coach's Clipboard

38. *Key Principle:* **A proper conditioning program is necessary to enjoying sports, and it is a keystone in lifelong fitness and good health.**

Coaching Strategy: Educate young athletes about the need for and the techniques of good conditioning. Take advantage of conditioning methods developed by exercise scientists and offer a comprehensive training program that focuses on improving athletes' body composition, flexibility, strength and power, endurance, and speed.

39. *Key Principle:* **Reducing body fat demands increasing training, which requires the expenditure of a significant amount of energy.**

Coaching Strategy: Plan and conduct a program of fatness reduction compatible with good health and effective training principles:

1. Calculate a specific goal of fatness level and determine what the body weight will be when that fatness level is achieved.
2. Decrease body-fat weight at a rate no more rapid than 2 or 3 pounds each week.
3. During early preseason conditioning, reduce the food intake of a typical high school or college-aged athlete to no less than approximately 2,000 kilocalories per day.
4. For the junior high school male, similarly restrict his intake to no less than 2,000 kilocalories, and strive to maintain a stationary weight through a program of conditioning exercises and a controlled diet.

40. *Key Principle:* **Paying attention to fatness level is a sound part of the conditioning program of all individuals regardless of sex or age.**

Coaching Strategy: Exercise involving regular expenditures of energy is the first essential to fatness control for everyone, not just athletes. Make a decision as to the goals of the program and how intensely involved a given individual will become in it.

41. *Key Principle:* **Achieving and controlling a desired body composition through a well-planned preseason conditioning program can provide one of the greatest health benefits of athletic participation.**

Coaching Strategy: Help athletes of both sexes to shape up for competition and thereby lay the foundation for lifelong fitness and good health.

42. *Key Principle:* **Flexibility may decrease the risk of injury and it does improve performance.**

Coaching Strategy: Give athletes instruction in sport-specific static flexibility exercises. Utilize the flexibility-maintenance routine presented on page 110.

43. *Key Principle:* **Proper strength training actually increases flexibility and enhances speed while increasing strength and power at the same time.**

Coaching Strategy: Develop and implement a strength training program to effectively condition the major muscle groups of the body. You can utilize a strengthening program that does not require any special muscle training apparatus or weight training facilities (see pages 112–113).

44. *Key Principle:* **In almost every high school and certainly in every metropolitan community, there are weight lifting gyms with strength conditioning programs that involve the use of elaborate and often very expensive equipment.**

Coaching Strategy: Supervise the utilization of weight training machines in accordance with the following points:

- Weight training apparatus should only be used with supervision and guidance of a knowledgeable coach.
- Improperly used equipment can be dangerous and harmful, particularly to the young athlete.
- To reduce the risk of injury, weights and weight training machines should be adjusted to fit the characteristics of the user.
- The results of weight training primarily depend on the effort that the athlete puts into the program.
- To avoid many of the risks of injury and poor results, athletes must adhere to the program on a regular basis.

45. *Key Principle:* **The athlete's ability to extract oxygen from the air and transport it to the muscles is known as his or her aerobic capacity, and the limits of this capacity vary among individuals.**

Coaching Strategy: Devise and implement a training program to increase athletes' aerobic capacity, or the endurance needed for moderate to long efforts. In so doing, use moderate-intensity exercises, such as distance running, prolonged swimming, or bicycle riding, over a long time period.

Coach's Clipboard

46. *Key Principle:* **The heart rate is a valid indicator of aerobic capacity and of how close to maximum the body is working to use oxygen.**

Coaching Strategy: Teach athletes to determine how close to maximum aerobic capacity they are exercising and how much potential for increase there may be with further training. Simply have them monitor their heart rates by following these procedures:

- Stretch and warm up very well.
- Run at a speed that can be continued for only 2 or 3 minutes.
- When you can't go any farther, slow down and count your pulse rate for 10 seconds. To determine maximal heart rate, multiplied this number by six.

47. *Key Principle:* **An effective conditioning program to improve aerobic capacity involves exercising at progressively greater levels of maximum aerobic capacity for relatively brief periods of time and performing such exercise repeatedly.**

Coaching Strategy: To improve aerobic capacity, follow the progressive exercise schedule outlined in Table 9.3 on page 117.

48. *Key Principle:* **Potentials for strength, quickness, coordination, intensity of effort, and interest all vary among individuals and all influence the conditioning response.**

Coaching Strategy: Emphasize to young athletes that the response to any conditioning effort will vary greatly among them (i.e., high degree of individuality). Be particularly understanding and reassuring during early explorations of physical conditioning.

49. *Key Principle:* **All experienced athletes know that the response in performance to overload is not proportional to the degree of overload.**

Coaching Strategy: To maximize the response to conditioning, regularly increase the intensity of the conditioning effort (i.e., the principle of overload). To reduce frustration and discouragement with the rate of progress, emphasize the individuality of the response to overload.

50. *Key Principle:* The muscles themselves and the nature of the work they are going to be asked to perform are all very specific to an individual's sport.

Coaching Strategy: Design practice activities to simulate the movements and activities involved in the particular sport. Utilize progressively more sport-specific conditioning programs as the competitive season comes closer.

51. *Key Principle:* More often than not, high school athletes are highly motivated to take part in a good conditioning program.

Coaching Strategy: Provide well-supervised preseason, in-season, and off-season conditioning programs for committed high school athletes who wish to see just what kind of new body can be developed.

52. *Key Principle:* As increasing millions of Americans begin to assume greater responsibility for their own health and fitness, conditioning programs and new fitness techniques become more important and popular.

Coaching Strategy: Encourage and reinforce youngsters' participation in conditioning programs. Help them to establish a serious commitment to lifelong fitness.

53. *Key Principle:* The young person freaked out on amphetamines is not going to be very competitive on any sport team.

Coaching Strategy: Give athletes information and counseling about the harmful effects of nervous-system stimulants:

- Exaggerated sense of performance enhancement.
- Reduced powers of perception.
- Disrupted fine motor coordination.
- Increased risk of injury.

54. *Key Principle:* Anabolic steroids will, in the long run, take their harmful toll.

Coaching Strategy: Warn athletes about the hazards/dangers associated with steroid use:

- Heart disease.
- Sexual and reproductive disorders.
- Immune deficiencies.
- Liver disorders.
- Stunted growth.
- Psychological disturbances.

55. *Key Principle:* Lyle Alzado, a star professional football player, campaigned against the use of anabolic steroids before his death from cancer, which was attributed to steroid effects.

Coaching Strategy: Counsel youngsters against the chemical "shortcuts" to strength and performance enhancement, and forbid their use. Moreover, the watchword is BEWARE.

56. *Key Principle:* Older and stronger athletes are more capable of causing injury to themselves and to their opponents.

Coaching Strategy: Develop a working/applied knowledge of specific injuries that commonly occur in your sport. Regardless of the athletes' age or level of competition, accept responsibility for the management of sport-related injuries, including procedures for their prevention, recognition, and treatment.

57. *Key Principle:* The most common sport-related injuries are the so-called overuse injuries, the too-much, too-soon, too-fast injuries.

Coaching Strategy: Vary practice and training regimens in terms of frequency, amount, duration, intensity, and specificity so that performance can still be enhanced but risk of overuse injuries reduced. In utilizing so-called periodization of training, provide the rest that various body structures need between periods of overload.

Coach's Clipboard

58. *Key Principle:* Never apply heat to a sports injury unless it is ordered by a physician.

Coaching Strategy: Promptly apply the only first-aid treatment that is safe for treatment of a sports injury without professional advice—***ICE***:

- **I** for ice.
- **C** for compression.
- **E** for elevation.

59. *Key Principle:* When properly applied, ICE treatments can do no harm to any type of injury.

Coaching Strategy: Promptly and repeatedly apply **ICE** treatments to significantly reduce the discomfort and period of limited activity resulting from an injury. Almost anything else—including heat applications—can cause harm in some instances.

60. *Key Principle:* Training in CPR (cardiopulmonary resuscitation) teaches the basic life-saving techniques that can keep a seriously injured athlete alive until emergency medical aid arrives.

Coaching Strategy: Be prepared for an emergency by getting certified in CPR. Use CPR if an accident or injury to an athlete results in any of the following symptoms:

- Not breathing.
- Unconscious.
- Bleeding
- In shock—particularly during hot weather.

61. *Key Principle:* Never encourage an athlete to play with pain, for there is a strong possibility of making the injury more serious.

Coaching Strategy: As a general rule, it is never appropriate to play an injured or ill youngster. Use common sense in making a decision to remove a youngster from a game, or to withhold an athlete from a practice or game. If you are uncertain about it, don't hesitate to seek input from a sports medicine specialist.

Part V

Coaching Challenges and How to Deal With Them

---

62. **Key Principle:** Sports can be a growth experience for problem athletes, but dealing with these athletes requires additional knowledge, understanding, and patience on the part of coaches.

    Coaching Strategy: The name of the game is flexibility. Being flexible does not mean having different rules for different athletes, any more than fairness means treating everyone exactly alike. Team rules must hold for everyone, or discipline and respect break down quickly. On the other hand, knowledge and respect for the makeup of each individual can be a key to successful coaching.

    1. *The uncoachable athlete:* The resistant athlete is frequently acting out unresolved problems with authority figures. He or she may need exposure to a firm yet caring coaching style.

    2. *The spoiled brat:* The spoiled brat needs to learn that no individual is more important that the team and that team goals take priority over individual goals. There are no special favors.

    3. *The low self-esteem child:* These athletes have an inferiority complex. The goal-setting and performance-feedback approaches described in Chapter 5 can be very helpful for such athletes, for they can clearly see the results of their efforts and can't write them off as being due to chance or luck. If you can help them learn to take pride in their efforts and their willingness to put themselves on the line, the sport experience can be a turning point for them.

    4. *The hyperanxious child:* These athletes become tense and "psyched out" in competition. You will recognize this pattern as the high-fear-of-failure athlete discussed in Chapter 6. Coaches can counter fear of failure by emphasizing effort and individual improvement and showing such athletes that they are never "losers" when they give it their best shot.

    5. *The withdrawn child:* The withdrawn athlete has often been hurt in previous relationships and fears getting close to others. Demonstrating that you care and gaining trust is critical.

63. **Key Principle:** Several thought-provoking questions can help parents understand their roles and responsibilities toward their young athletes and avoid interference with your coaching.

Coaching Strategy: Some thought provoking questions for parents include:
1. Can the parents give up their child? This requires putting the child in your charge and trusting you to guide his or her sport experience.
2. Can the parents admit their shortcomings? Parents must be convinced that the proper response to a mistake or not knowing something is an honest disclosure.
3. Can the parents accept their child's triumphs?
4. Can the parents accept their child's disappointments?
5. Can the parents give their child some time?
6. Can the parents let their child make his or her own decisions?
7. Can the parents show their child self-control?

64. **Key Principle:** Acceptable standards for spectator behavior should be firmly communicated to parents for the purpose of preventing problems at competitive events.

Coaching Strategy:
1. Parents should remain seated in the spectator area during the contest.
2. Parents should not yell instructions or criticisms to the children.
3. Parents should make no derogatory comments to players, parents of the opposing team, officials, or league administrators.
4. Parents should not interfere with their children's coach.

65. **Key Principle:** Communication is the key to friendly, productive relations with parents.

Coaching Strategy: Parents have both the right and the responsibility to inquire about all activities that their children are involved in, including sports. They should take this responsibility seriously, probing into the nature and quality of specific sport programs. Tell parents of your willingness to discuss any problems that might arise. Let them know that you are open to receiving their input. If you keep the lines of communication open, you will be more likely to have constructive relations with parents. There is, however, a proper time and place for interaction with you. That time is not during a practice or a contest, and it is not in the presence of youngsters. Tell parents what times and places are best suited for discussions with you.

66. **Key Principle:** There are effective ways of dealing with disinterested, over-critical, excessively vocal, meddling, and overprotective parents.

Coaching Strategy:
1. *Disinterested Parents:* Talk to the child and ask if the lack of parental involvement troubles him or her.
2. *Overcritical Parents:* Some parents unconsciously equate the success or fail-ure of their child with their own success or failure. You should attempt to make overcritical parents aware of this problem as tactfully as possible.
3. *Parents who scream from behind the bench:* Do not get into an argument with a screaming parent. It will not do any good and will probably make things worse. During a break in the contest (half-time, between periods), ask other parents or league administrators to calmly and tactfully point out to the person that such yelling is a poor example to the young athletes.
4. *Sideline Coaches:* Advise your athletes that during practices and contests you are the coach and that you want their full attention. Tell the parent pri-vately how confusing it is for the athletes when two or more people are telling them what to do.
5. *Overprotective Parents:* You must try to eliminate the fear of injury by reas-suring the parent that the event is fairly safe. Explain the rules and equipment that protect the athletes. Point out how good coaching, program administration, and officiating add to the safety of the sport.

67. **Key Principle:** With sufficient planning and preparation, a preseason coach-parent meeting can be an enjoyable experience.

Coaching Strategy: Use the guidelines on pages 159–165.

Index

actions, coach's example 9–10
aversive control 25
awards 173

Bill of Rights for Young Athletes 11–12
body characteristics 92–94
    genetic factors 93
    of today's athlete 104

CET (Coach Effectiveness Training™) definition of; effects on athletes; effects on coach behaviors; effects on dropout rates; increasing self esteem; reducing performance anxiety; research in 28–30
character 8–9, 13
coach (roles of) 23
Coach Self–Report Form 47
coaching guidelines, summary of 46–48
coaching, psychology of 24–25
communication 44–45
competition, boys vs. girls 99
conditioning programs 118–120
    individualized programs 120–23
cutting, kids from a team 168–69

developmental model, of sports 13
disciplinary problems 170–71
discipline 38–41
drugs 123–26

family life, and coaching 175–76
fear 25–27
fear of failure 27, 31, 66–68
fun 14–15

goals 53–53
    long–range goals 53
    outcome goals 54
    performance goals 54
    pitfalls 57
    short–range goals 53
goals achievement strategies 55–56
goal–setting 51–59
growth 99–100

injury 127
    do's 130–31
    don'ts 129–30
    emergencies 133–34
    prevention 131–33
    severity of 134

legal suits, ways to avoid 135–38
losing (a game) 171–72

mental imagery 81–87
mental toughness 65–79
misbehavior (of coaches) 174
mistakes, positive approach to 35–38
moral behavior, sportsmanship 9–10
motivation 51

negative approach, to coaching; definition of 25

organized sports, reasons for
participating in 14
own child coaching 174–75

parental behavior 154
parents
communications with 154–55
preseason meeting with 158–65
problem behaviors of 155–58
roles and responsibilities 149–54
performance feedback
(goal evaluation) 56
physical abilities 97–99
childhood 97
adolescence 97–99
physical growth 94–97
sex differences 96–97
physical maturity 100–04
early maturer 101–03
late maturer 103–04
play 3–4
positive approach, to coaching,
definition of 25
positive control 25
problem athletes 141–48
hyperanxious child 146–47
low self–esteem child 145–46
spoiled brat 144–45
uncoachable child 142–44
withdrawn child 147–48
professional model (of sports) 12–13
punishment 26–27

quitting (kids from a team) 169–70

reinforcement, definition of 32
reinforcement principles 33–35
relaxation 75–79
respect 167–68

self–awareness 44–46
skill 51
sport skills, teaching of 43–44
sportsmanship 9
stress 61–62
athletic stress, effects of 62–65
reducing stress 66–79
success 15–17, 51

team rules 39–40
team rule violations 40–41
team unity 41–43
training 105–18
body composition 106–109
endurance 114–17
flexibility 109–11
speed 117–18
strength 111–14

winning 14–18, 31
philosophy of winning 17–18
winning (a game) 172–73

youth sports
history of 4–5
pros and cons 6–8
size 4

Performance Enhancement Services

Performance Enhancement Services offers three sport psychology programs for coaches, parents, and athletes:
- Coach Effectiveness Training
- Parent Sport Orientation
- Psychological Skills Training

Coach Effectiveness Training (CET) is a 2.5-hour workshop designed to improve coach-athlete interactions and thereby increase the value of sport participation for athletes' personal, social, and athletic development. Way to Go, Coach! is the text for CET, which is the only coaching education program that is based on scientific studies of coaching behaviors and their effects on young athletes. More than 17,000 youth sport coaches have participated in CET workshops presented in the United States and Canada. CET has also been included in inservice training for PE teachers and coaches in public school districts.

Parent Sport Orientation (PSO) is a 1.5-hour workshop for parents of young athletes. The overall objective is to improve parents' understanding of youth sports. The specific purposes are to (a) identify and clarify the objectives of youth sports, (b) educate parents about their roles and responsibilities relative to their youngsters' participation in sports, and (c) establish clear lines of communication between parents and coaches. PSO has been sponsored by youth sport organizations and by parent-teacher-student associations.

Psychological Skills Training (PST) is designed to help athletes to control mental and emotional factors that affect how well and how consistently they perform. "Mental toughness" training involves learning a set of performance enhancement skills that can be applied both on and off the athletic field/court—goal setting, attention control/concentration, stress management, mental rehearsal. PST has been provided for individual athletes, teams, and coaches. Training programs are also available for business and industry.

Ronald E. Smith and **Frank L. Smoll** are Co-Directors of Performance Enhancement Services. For more information on the programs, call (206) 543-4612.

Warde Publishers, Inc.

for additional copies of

Way to Go, Coach!

A Scientifically Proven Approach
to Youth Sports Coaching Effectiveness

Write:

Warde Publishers, Inc.
3000 Alpine Road
Portola Valley, CA 94028

Toll-free order line: (800) 699–2733

ORDER FORM

Please send me _____ copy(ies) of *Way to Go, Coach!* A Scientifically Proven Approach to Youth Sports Coaching Effectiveness by Ronald E. Smith and Frank L. Smoll at $17.95. (Add $4.50 for first copy and $.50 for each additional copy for packing and shipping. California residents, add $1.48 sales tax per book ordered.) Make check payable to Warde Publishers, Inc.

Total Enclosed = $ _____

Name _____

Organization _____

Address _____

City _____ State _____ Zip _____

May we send information on *Way to Go, Coach!* to a colleague or associate?

Referral name _____

Organization _____

Address _____

City _____ State _____ Zip _____

☐ Please send information on other titles in the Coaching Education series.